Rodney

Now is Your

Your PATH is

Now You Rock!!

Time To Fly

Motivated Publishing
STUDIOS

How to GIVE Birth to a KONDOR

By: Tony Lucero

Published by: *Motivated Publishing Studios*

Tony Lucero
tonylucero.com

ISBN: 978-0-692-88255-9

Printed in the USA
First Edition, June 2017

Edited by: Rory d'Eon
Proofreading by: RD
Interior layout by: Rod Schulhauser
Project Management by: Motivated Publishing Studios

Dedications

For my wife, who is the highest representation of love in my life. She encouraged me daily to leave the nest so that I could "glide" and discover.

To all the people that have touched, taught, shared, guided, inspired and spent a portion of their time with me no matter how long it took, this book is dedicated to you, for in our connection, I grew and became who I am today.

To my family, despite me being a tad "different," I applaud your patience with me, especially Mom.

To a true teacher of life, Mallku, who opened my heart, my spirit and wings, so I could continue my mission.

And finally, to Jonas, my friend from the Amazon, I know you are laughing from above.

Table of Contents

Dedications • iii

Acknowledgments • vii

Foreword • ix

Preface • xi

Choice • 1

Change • 9

The Sound of Music • 15

Gut Check • 19

Teach Me • 27

Law of Manifestation • 35

Mirror, Mirror on the Wall • 45

Don't be a Twinkie • 57

Growth is Good • 61

I was Runnnnninggg! • 73

It's Alive • 83

The Call • 87

It's a Question of Love • 95

Set Me Free • 99

This Isn't It • 105

Let the Healing Begin • 113

Peru • 119

- The Beginning of Something Big • 120
- A Magical Place • 125
- Becoming a Lion • 131
- Sharing the Magic • 135

Get Back in the Game • 139

The Sequel, Peru Again • 143

- A Wandering Beginning • 146
- A Better Place • 149
- The Gift • 152

Born Again • 157
I Felt Me • 158
Becoming a Kondor • 162
Connected • 164
Breaking Free • 168

APPENDIX • 173
How to Give Birth to a Kondor • 173
My Greatest Gift • 176
My Gift to the World • 178
Living in Your Circles of Your Life • 179
Experiences • 180
Wellness • 180
Prosperity • 181
Taking a Time Out • 182
A Few Final Words • 185
Reminders • 186
Kondor Notes • 187

Acknowledgments

I have many amazing people to thank. Many are mentioned in this book. I'm very grateful for their insights and support.

My whole life, I've been guided by an energy and spirit that continues to do wonderful work for me.

As a child, I was connected to Pachamama's (Mother Earth) energy. Now, as a man, I'm reminded each and every day that her power is nothing short of miraculous. To my spirit master, Pachakamaq, the spirit of the universe that governs all the changes we see and feel, I honor your willingness to encourage much needed change on our planet. To Wiraqocha, the essence of life and creator of our reality (of what we see on this planet), I welcome the new reality you have given me.

To everyone who has encouraged me to write a story and assisted me to the end and beyond, I honor each of you.

I know that the people who follow me make me a better leader. Your will to keep going, no matter what, is my inspiration to be a better version of myself. Every connection I have made has enabled me to grow. If we have ever crossed paths, our gathering is something I'll always cherish.

Finally, I want to acknowledge all of you for taking time away from your life to get to know mine. I know that if we ever meet, it will be like souls reconnecting.

I have shared a part of me with you. My wish is that you take and share part of you with the world. We need to hear your story too!

With gratitude, beauty and love,

Tony Lucero

Foreword

Tony is giving a deep key to open your personal unveiled doors to your inner peace and realization. This book is taking you on a personal adventure beyond time with the purpose of showing your own beauty and strength.

Becoming a Kondor is the path of rebirth for manifesting your mission on Earth.

Mallku,
Author of the books: *The Awakening of the Puma*, *The Crystal City of Machu Pijchu*, *Cusco Forever*, and *Inka Power Places*.

Preface

The idea of writing a book came up many times in my life. I'd get started and say, "This is not it." I have five books in production that are "Not it."

Certain things needed to come to fruition. When they did, this book resulted.

This is far more than a book of personal development, this is a guide to personal discovery and finding your purpose. Within these chapters, you'll see moments of my life, perhaps even moments of your life, that offer an opportunity to reflect, an opportunity to understand, and yes, an opportunity for personal development.

As I looked back on my life and the sequence of certain events and the experience I gained from those events, it dawned on me that inside these life lessons were the ingredients for someone to become "activated." By this, I mean when someone becomes activated their life will be different from that moment forward.

This is far deeper than a wake-up call. When you become activated, you begin to discover your special talents, skills, powers and energies in a way you've never felt before. You don't settle for smallness any longer. You begin to see, and more importantly feel, what a limitless life can be like.

You can't sleep because you're on a path of discovery. You want to become a master. You now know you'll become untouchable, hatching out of the life you once knew.

I wrote this book at the time when I discovered *the* formula after many years of trial and error. My life is dedicated to the mission of helping others activate and discover a more purposeful life.

There's more to this book than just reading it—there's work to be done too. At the end of each chapter I include my life lesson. You, my friend, will be asked to participate and complete an exercise before you move on. This is not a book with CliffsNotes. The life you desire is going to take some time and some *good* (work).

This book is a symbol of my life and will become an integral part of your life's path. The blueprint included is well proven. The life you seek will not take the 50 years it took me. Read it slowly, do the *good* and implement daily what you're learning and feeling.

The journey to your birth is certainly worth it. And I can assure you that your wind is coming. All you'll need to do then is stretch your wings and glide.

Let's discover together. May you find the true meaning of Munay as you fly!

1

Choice

"The best choice is to exercise your freedom of choice."

That old saying, "You can't choose your parents," is true in my life.

My given name is Anthony. I was born in September 1966, and like you, I was unable to choose my parents. The name "Anthony" never quite resonated with me. It was only used when my mother had an issue with my behavior, therefore I quickly associated the name with something Mom didn't like. For that reason, I went by Tony, but always referred to myself as "Tony the Tiger."

My father was born in the Philippines, my mom in Minnesota. She started having children at a young age. In total, three of us: two boys and a girl.

I was the middle child, the child that loved the sun and had the personality of a comedian on Ritalin. I was the fun, happy kid that could do no wrong. While still young, my personality enabled me to turn any situation into something that was cute or no big deal. I'm still very young at heart and have retained the use of those powers developed so long ago. I soaked in the love my mom gave me, even though life would become more difficult with what was to follow.

At the age of seven, my parents divorced. Later, my mother married the man that became the biggest motivator in my life. Because of him, I never quit. I remained on my path of discovery, no matter what.

Seeing that last sentence, you're probably thinking, "Wow, I wish I had a mentor like that, a father who was like him."

George was a big powerful Portuguese man that worked in Salinas, California as a foreman for a construction company. Broad shoulders, big voice, callused hands and one rule—his. The fact we were our mother's baggage only made living under his rule more difficult.

We could do no right. Threats, yelling, and belittling was our daily fare. All of us, kids and Mom alike, were afraid of him. For the longest time, I thought my name was Jesus Christ, something he'd yell at me from the next room. "Jesus Christ, get your ass in here!"

Have I mentioned my name is Tony? I would even have accepted Anthony at that point. As a young child, the last thing you want to hear is language describing you as stupid, and someone who shouldn't even try because failure is inevitable. Nothing I did was enough or right. "What's wrong with you? Can't you do anything right?" Aren't they words that just fill your heart? So how was I, a kid with a father like that, supposed to cope?

I had to teach myself some valuable lessons. The first one: Use my imagination.

I became a superhero, of sorts. I had to get lost in my imagination to separate myself from the current situation. I had to make my reality distinctly separate from his. In a sense, I put myself in a movie.

So how is this possible for a kid my age? Kids have imagination. I had imagination. Using it, I was able to find a safe place, a place in which to get lost and create my own reality.

I would play in the Eucalyptus forest where I lived, pretending I was a superhero. We superheroes have special powers. So, no matter how much mental, and sometimes physical, damage he inflicted, I survived. I had literally developed the power to make his harsh words, his hate, anger, frustration and my fear disappear.

Even at that young age, I'd discovered that humans have the ability and the power, if we so choose, to tap into something far more transcendent than what we normally use, and summon it the instant we need it. As a kid, I used my imagination to get lost in my new reality because it felt better than remaining in his, or someone else's. I was able to choose my state and in any given moment choose another. Best of all, we all have this ability.

The question you need to understand is, do you willingly exercise this power? The power of "choice" and "imagination" can transport you to places you've never been, allow you to see farther, do more, and experience more. I'm convinced not using either of these gifts has led to more deaths than any disease known to man. Use your power of choice. Don't let the moments of yesterday affect the moments of today.

So how did this wisdom come to me at such an early age? I believe that we, all of us, are destined to something purposeful. I believed that how George was making me feel, the descriptions he used for me, were not my reality, but only his. Could I really be all these terrible things? Was I really stupid? Worthless? A mistake? I chose not to believe him.

I chose using my imagination. It provided a better version of life than what was available. It removed me from the situation.

As a seven-year-old, I had no bank account, rich uncle, driver's license, car, or knowledge of life. I chose to use my imagination to create my own superhero movie, be the director, writer, producer and of course, the award-winning actor.

I got so good at it, that every time George would raise his voice to threaten me, I would just smile (inside only, as he had heavy hands) and get ready to don my cape of "reflection." It was my choice. And it enabled me to get through the most difficult times.

That was when I was seven. My life had only just begun. Now I have more than 43 years of experience to share. So, if you don't mind, I'd like to introduce you to the first activity designed to help find your superpowers of choice and imagination.

This is one that you must do right now, without hesitation. The longer you wait, the more opportunity there is for things to sneak in and do damage. This damage, compounded day after day, month after month, will make it difficult for you to use this power in the future, as there are also other powerful forces that welcome the weak. But, this is not you; it never was.

Today, you're a person with choice and imagination. You choose your feelings, your action and reactions, your words, and your direction. You, and you alone, have been given this, the mightiest of all powers—choice. Remember the moment you felt negative energy pulling you down, dragging you through the mud, your heart slowly slipping, and you immediately made a "choice" to change? The motivational guru's call this change a pattern interrupt. The interruption changes your state.

Let's put this into practice.

Spend a few moments, no longer than 18 minutes, to create the life you choose. Choose your friends, your environment, health, attitude, wisdom, materials, etc. You get the idea.

For example:

- I choose to have love in my life for family and friends.
- I choose energy.
- I choose positivity over negativity.
- I choose healthy eating.
- I choose happiness.
- I choose loving myself.
- I choose 30 minutes of exercise daily.
- I choose chocolate.
- Etc.

Create your unique list using the following pages. Get your imagination fired up—you only have 18 minutes. Set your clock, create your list and do NOT move forward. The combination, sequence and activity outlined here is very important. This list becomes your armor. It will protect you from the elements. The more you use your power of choice, the more the negative elements will leave you alone and find a weaker bystander. Have this list readily available; you'll need it very soon, I can assure you. Life is like that.

Remember, you chose me. We're partners, making sure everything is done correctly. You're a superhero, one with many unique powers that we're going to reveal—all for your benefit. No skipping forward or you'll break the sequence I've created and weaken the trust. Make a "choice" to do the exercise. You'll love what comes with those choices. See you at the next lesson.

I choose ____

I choose ____

I choose ____

I choose ____

I choose ____

I choose ____

I choose ____

I choose ____

I choose ____

I choose ____

I choose ____

I choose ____

I choose ____

I choose ____

I choose ____

I choose ____

I choose ____

I choose ____

I choose ____

I choose ____

I choose ____

I choose ____

I choose ____

I choose ____

I choose ____

2

Change

"You are able to navigate the direction of your life."

Change is good; that's a fact.

My mother, an amazing woman, had an issue with finding the right man. Her quest for love was an admirable goal, but after five marriages it became tough on all of us.

After five years, George and his constant abuse became too much, so mother planned our escape. One morning, after he'd left for work, a moving van pulled up to the house and we began tossing our belongings—just necessities—into boxes. We followed that van all the way to Houston, Texas, and moved in with her brother.

By that time, we were five in all—her and four kids. Our family had grown. George and Mom had a son together.

George Jr. was now two. I was 11, my older brother 12, and my sister was eight.

It was during this time, approaching middle school, that I became comfortable with change and being forced to adapt to new situations. My clothing was different, so was my language and vibe.

Kids can be tough on other kids and I got my share. Words like queer and gay were new to me. But directed at me, I quickly figured them out. However, this was their reality, not mine, thanks to my superhero powers.

Over time, I adapted to a certain pseudo Cal/Tex style of dress and added "ya'll" to my vocabulary. To this day, I still say ya'll.

All this change was me adapting to my surroundings, making changes that made my world more comfortable. Seeking comfort in everything we do is a human trait.

Adaptation is a skill that simplifies your life. I'm not saying give in, I'm saying adapt. Subtle adjustments provide comfort without sacrificing values. Change is essential, part of evolution, part of life.

Everything around us changes—time, the weather, leaves on the trees, the tide, the current situation, you name it. Life without change is death. Coming to terms with that sobering thought, especially when we feel stuck and have no exit plan, forces us to become comfortable with change.

Over time, we change our fashion, our eating habits, our relationships, where we live, our careers and much more. I'm not trying to point out the obvious here, but rather I want you to think about how change comes to you.

In the last chapter, we talked about choice. The moment a choice is made, certain energies come into play. Change exists in that choice—it's inevitable. What happens next is—obviously—your choice.

If I say I'm going on vacation then immediately change what happens next—like going online and picking a location, a date, doing research, or booking a room—I've altered the outcome. I have put change into action.

My mother, for the longest time, talked about moving. We discussed it like a covert operation. However, nothing was done. There were too many logistical problems, the timing was never good, and she was fearful of both staying and going. It took an especially violent night to trigger the move.

We were fortunate to be able to leave without being harmed. But once on our way, our family was on a new path. Our change was affected by our action. It wasn't just time for change, it was time to *act* on the change that was necessary.

I hope that, after all that, you understand that change is necessary for activation. Change in one area out of many will not only be welcome, but in most cases will instantly change the frequency, or flow, of your current situation. You'll begin to vibrate at another level—one that's intoxicating. The idea of change and choice becomes your aphrodisiac for a better life. Have you ever made a decision then said, "Wow, I'm so glad I did that!"?

What took you so long? So, embrace change. Don't get lost in yesterday's movie. Focus on the moment. Tune into what you're feeling now and think in terms of change.

When change is needed, you'll know. However, where we often fall short is making the choice to go ahead and make that change.

But you're not like that. You've made an investment in this book—you've already decided to choose and change. It feels good to be in charge. You're not going to wait until you're not well, or the planets align in a certain way, or, in my case, life at home is fraught with danger.

The lesson here is to ask yourself, "What needs to change, right now?" Pick that which has been nagging at you the longest. Or pick something that's taking up valuable time or causing discomfort or disease.

Take a few moments to write this down. This shouldn't take very long. What mechanism or strategy should be put into motion—right now—to make these changes happen? Write out the steps.

I'll wait for you to finish.

What is the one change that needs to occur right now ?

What good will come from this change ?

3

The Sound of Music

"Everything has a frequency and a beat."

This might be an interesting chapter—a surprise. As a child living in a hostile household, there were certain periods of peace. One thing my mother instilled in us was the need to learn music. Music is universal. Music is food for the soul. She knew this.

Around my seventh year, I was told that I had to learn to play an instrument. I had no choice. I chose the guitar and began lessons.

It quickly became apparent that I had an ear for music. I learnt quickly, understood the concept of notes, and could play by ear, figuring things out by myself.

Music makes us dance, cry, love, laugh, feel and remember. Music alters our current state and evokes concentration. It's an outlet and expression of character. In my view, it's essential to foster a connection between music and self. Later, I'll show you how it impacted my life and enabled me to reach out to others to enlighten their lives.

It's no secret that music can heal and alter one's state to achieve phenomenal results.

Here's how to do this for yourself: Learn to play a musical instrument.

You're never too old; it's never too late. Dedicate 15 to 30 minutes a few times a week to learning the flute, the kazoo, a harmonica, anything. The idea is to stretch, to discover something new in yourself. Don't lie and say you have no talent.

Just as a friendly reminder, you're still that better version of yourself—don't revert to yesterday's chatter. After all, we've heard you singing in the car, beating on the steering wheel while Steve Perry from Journey blares *Don't Stop Believing* on the radio. So, what instrument should you take up?

Make it easy on yourself. Pick any instrument and go to YouTube. Search for videos that teach you how to play and away you go.

Everyone deserves a creative outlet. Playing an instrument is the best thing you can do to free your soul and enable that connection with something larger than yourself.

Music is the only medium that connects people to each other and to Mother Earth. Plus, you'll be surrounded with music for the rest of your life. So, go ahead, give it a try.

Write this down:

- When are you getting an instrument?

____

- What's the first song you'll play?

____

Music is now your lifelong friend. Play loud and proud!

What instrument did you choose ?

When are your practice sessions ?

4

Gut Check

"The quality of life is an inside job."

Let's go forward in time a bit, to when I was seventeen. Up to that point I had a pretty normal life, once we were removed from you-know-who's grasp.

I was athletic. I excelled at basketball, tennis and baseball. I loved theatre, which satisfied my creative energy. I also fell in love, many times, so I thought. I played in a band for a while, entered music talent shows and had great relationships with my teachers. I was that kid that lit up a room with a smile engraved on my face.

I had superpowers. I used and honed them every day. No one knew of this, of course. Superheroes remain incognito until needed. You'll see what I mean when you begin using your superpowers or help others discover theirs.

In my senior year, 1984, I became a man. My mom was raising the three of us by herself. George insisted George Jr. live with him, so while we lived in Houston, Jr. stayed in California. More on this later. Right then, I was in love with my high school sweetheart, Raquel.

As summer approached, I began asking myself what I would do after graduation. Mom was keeping the family together by herself. Money was tight; college was out of the question. Anyway, school was more of a social experiment than anything else. So I made a decision that no one else in my senior year made—I enlisted.

I joined the United States Air Force in December 1984, and quickly got shipped off to Lackland Air Force Base in San Antonio, Texas.

As the bus pulled in I wondered, "What the heck did I just do?" Six weeks basic training would strain my superpowers to the limit. With this movie, I would surely win my Oscar. The decision to enlist would ultimately deliver some of my most defining life lessons.

I was 18, not dependent on my mother for cooking and cleaning, cash or daily guidance. It was a big step for me, since I still defined myself as a kid. But I was bulletproof. I'd been to war, figuratively, many times before. I was battle-tested and ready. How hard could basic training be?
Somehow, I had become comfortable with the adaptation. In my mind, I truly felt I was in my next Hollywood production. However, this one brought me right back to my days with George.

In the military, especially in basic training, soldiers don't use loving voices to get their points across. There's a constant barrage of yelling, stomping of feet, more yelling, more stomping, belittling, and general chaos and high intensity. This all reminded me of George.

How many times in your past have you been transported back because of some action or situation? Those feelings you thought buried spring right up. I spent six weeks reliving my childhood.

But I had to stay in the moment. I had to draw upon my powers and keep on my chosen path. The chaos and yelling was their reality, not mine. I was merely portraying a role in a movie of my own choosing. My decision. My issue. And I would be fine in the end.

On day one, I learned I was not a very good follower. Military regulations are insane. They dictate what your hair looks like, what you wear, when you can leave, where you go. There are regulations for *everything*. All part of *their* master plan—not mine.

Don't get me wrong, the military was one of the best decisions I ever made. But it's not my cup of tea, long-term. I learned what I needed in order to survive. Actually, I did well, moving quickly up the ranks. Once I adjusted to military life, I began to plan my exit strategy.

During basic training, Raquel and I stayed together as best we could. Then I was transferred to Malmstrom AFB, Montana, as a Security Policeman. This was a crazy situation for someone who considered himself a lover, not a fighter. Lovers aren't supposed to carry an M-16 to work. But as an actor in my movie, I gave my best performance.

One morning, I got a call from Raquel. She wanted to *be* with me, not stay *away* and *separate*. So my movie became a romance too. She moved from Houston to Montana. We found an apartment and she got a job at a local hotel. We were still kids playing dress up, knowing little about marriage. But we had to have that conversation.

In the military, married couples get an allowance. So, in the name of getting that allowance—not so much for love—we decided to get married. We were married by a justice of the peace. I was 21.

It was a quick 15-minute ceremony, no honeymoon. So romantic. Those were *my* choices, but they allowed me to learn a huge lesson a few years later. You see, every choice alters something. It also unveils an opportunity for growth. I was about to grow, then get hit on the head by a freight train of emotion.

Raquel and I did quite well. But the desire to leave the military grew. I had received from the military what I'd come for. I had learned discipline, learned how to pay attention to detail, learned respect, honor, values, friendship, mission and team work. I could even fold my underwear in a six-inch perfect square.

I hold the utmost respect for what the military teaches a young person who wants to be part of a community and of a brotherhood that stands for something. But I had outgrown my decision. I needed to discover more about myself. However, those lessons the military taught me, I carried into my next adventure movie. I'm proud of my military years.

So, let's go over the lessons I learned.

The decision to leave the military, and the decisions that followed, were "gut" decisions. I had followed my gut when I joined, even when my head had told me, "You don't like guns, war, rules and dictatorships."

My gut countered by insisting I would learn something useful for later in life. I would relieve some of my mother's stress. And I might travel the world.

You can see, and feel, the tension between gut and head. However, my gut is the calmer, more loving voice.

Your mind plays so many different tapes and draws upon so many different sources, it creates doubt, uncertainty, procrastination, and much more. It's like a computer processing millions of information bits every second. Calling on your brain in times of change is easy, but NOT recommended.

Better to ask your brain to process all the information then ask your gut to make a choice based on that information. That way, your choice is based on feeling, not meaning.

Have you ever had the feeling to do something? To call someone? To go somewhere? And when you acted upon that feeling, did something beautiful happen?

Maybe you just had to leave a party and something better came up because you left. Did you run into an old friend? Did something truly wonderful happen?

Being in tune with your gut is empowering. It's a practice that you must not only recognize, but also put to constant use. It's a muscle that must be both stronger and louder than the brain.

The brain is perfect for information processing and controlling bodily functions. But it tends to confuse, sabotage and make you question what you *know* and *feel*.

When faced with a life-changing decision, you must follow your gut. It always knows best. The more in tune you are with it, the more dependable and reliable this power is. And the more you call upon it, the more confident you'll become to use it to handle difficult situations.

It's there to protect you, to soothe your choices and allow you an opportunity to have an experience that your mind has denied you. And now, you're at a stage in your life where your gut wants you to experience what comes next. It wants you to enjoy what's coming—to embrace it.

But, your brain is saying, "Wait until the end of the book." Don't. Ask your gut this question right now: "What does my gut, my center, my soul, want me to do right now?"

With that in mind, get pen and paper, put your left hand on your solar plexus, close your eyes and ask, "What is the most important thing I need to do, to experience, today?"

Write it down.

Congratulations, you've defied science and gone straight to the source for your first answer.

Now, no matter what, you must DO what you wrote. Put your plan into action. Get it done. Use your brain to prepare, but stay true to your gut's desire. Your gut is your new friend. It has been waiting patiently to point you to a life of possibilities and abundance. Admire your brain's power, but allow your gut's instinct to be the guide to life's maze.

Be proud of yourself. I'm proud of you. And I'm here with you. Together, we can get so much more out of life. But you haven't seen anything yet. There's so much more.

In the meantime, practice listening to your gut—every day. Any time you're unsure of yourself, listen closely to your gut. Later in the book, you'll meet and get handed off to the master teacher for your gut!

So now that you're ready and strong for what you're about to learn, let's move to the next chapter.

5

Teach Me

"Find your way by getting out of the way."

As Raquel and I began our transition from the military, we searched for different places to go. I'd spent most of my life in California, so I picked a city close to my mom. At the time, this was Santa Maria. Raquel stayed behind, working to save a few more dollars and spend time with her mother.

I'd saved enough for a house. After buying one, I began my search for a job. Santa Maria didn't offer much. It was a farming community. But, one day, an ad caught my eye. It offered a six-figure income, free training, unlimited growth, and promised to provide all my sales leads. It sounded like a good opportunity.

I put on a suit, showed up at their office, and was promptly escorted to a spacious back room set up as a classroom. Left and right, sat vacuum cleaners. I was going to be a dirt-sucking salesman! I was flabbergasted.

This guy Greg introduced himself as the owner, addressing about a dozen of us. He told us the Kirby story and how this Home Maintenance System had no competition. For the right people, it could generate five to eight thousand dollars a month, which could lead to a management position. He went on about how all our leads were provided and we just had to go demo the units—$2,250 vacuum cleaners…I mean Home Maintenance System.

At the end of his presentation, I thanked him for the opportunity. I'd let him know if I was interested. However, he still wanted to hire me. My military history had won him over.

I went home feeling dirty (pun intended). I felt like I'd been taken in by a bait-and-switch routine. In bed, unsure what to do, I decided to consult my gut. What did it feel I should do? My answer came immediately, one which overrode my brain's decision just hours earlier. Greg was going to get a wake-up call the next morning that would either excite him or piss him off.

I showed up just after they opened, in jeans, polo shirt and tennis shoes, and asked to speak to Greg. We made small talk then I got right to the point. "Greg," I said, "I've entertained the idea of being part of the Kirby story, but I'll only do so if you're open to a slight change to your hiring process."

I asked him who the top producer was, and after he told me (the man's name was Barry), I wanted Greg to assign that person to train me. I wanted to learn from the best.

Apparently, Barry was a bit of a legend. He sold more Kirbys than anyone. But he seldom was seen actually selling. He had his own schedule and his own system. But I wanted Barry as my teacher. I promised Greg I would not disappoint him and not waste Barry's time.

Barry generated his own leads, cold-calling door-to-door. He didn't rely on the office's leads. That way, he had control over the kind of people he targeted. And he targeted the rich.

If he entered a home, he sold a system. And he sold them for cash, not financed like most of the office did. He'd pack three machines into his Grand Torino and be sold out by 2 pm. He was a bona fide legend.

But Greg had doubts that Barry would agree. Working by himself, and successful, was too good a system to mess up. But Greg agreed to ask and I left knowing I had listened to my gut and presented my proposal with confidence. I was ready. It took three days for Greg to call with news. I played hard to get, delaying our meeting until the next morning, before office hours.

Barry was 6' 2" and 140 pounds, tops. His appearance—rail thin and topped by a golden, curly afro—shocked me. He looked old, dressed like it was still the 60s, chain-smoked, and loved faded gold-plated jewelry. If this guy was a legend, I would crush it!

We agreed to a one-week trial. If it didn't work out, we would part ways.

I spent the morning dismantling and reassembling the system Barry's way. Then I packed it up, his way, and that was it. The rest of my training would be on the road. With three systems in his smoke-infested car, we headed for the high-end homes and hills of money awaiting us.

At this stage, I was to watch but not speak unless the homeowner asked me a direct question. Once inside, he began with a script that never wavered. He moved easily, with grace (Who knew he could do this?) and had the customer saying "Yes," over and over—a good thing to hear when selling.

In less than 45 minutes, he collected a check for $2100 from the maid—not the homeowner! If Barry could sell to household staff, he was beyond good.

At lunch, we talked about that sale. From that conversation, and the sale itself, came several important lessons.

What made Barry so special was his ability to trust his own system, his process. The machine would always do its part. From waking onward, he was into his routine.

Everything, from what he wore, the time he arrived at the office, to when he headed out, was calculated. The pitch at the door never changed, and neither did his close. It was a system he'd perfected over years of selling.

I was rather curious about his dress choices. He told me that he made adjustments based on the income level of his audience—the higher the income, the better the clothes. But he also told me he dressed that way to create conversation, to seem less fortunate from a financial point of view and appear less threatening

He also knew his audience really well. He kept records of everyone he sold to—names he could use to sell another system.

In all, he was a true master.

In the short term, I became second in sales only to Barry. And before I left the company, I had become their top salesperson. However, all was not *that* rosy.

Because of my constant exposure to dust and dirt from the many demonstrations, I became sick. My edge slipped too. But I had learned some valuable lessons for my next adventure.

Two months into my sales job, I was given an opportunity to manage a crew of three. I was to train and help close their deals. They'd demo, I'd close.

It began like this: Greg called me one day saying one of his sales guys, Darren, was having some challenges selling. This, after two successful years. He'd just experienced three bad months and his marriage, and his life in general, was suffering. So I told Greg I'd help Darren get back on track.

Darren was actually very good. His demo was smooth, conversation with the homeowners was unforced, and he appeared to be enjoying it. But come time to close the sale, he became awkward. Everything about him changed: his words, his confidence, physiology, all of it.

Two demos later, I knew this was how it went every time. At that point, I decided we should talk. I told Darren that he did everything by the book. From a demo standpoint, he could have been the company's training video. Something else was wrong.

This is where things got emotional. Sharing details about home life and finances is never easy. When they're unpleasant, it's much worse. Much of his home conversation now revolved around money, not love or friendship. His marriage was failing, and he'd gained fifty pounds.

The pressure to sell at every single demo was intense. And, as we all know, humans can sense desperation. We can feel another's intentions (especially if in tune with your gut). His clients sensed the insincerity. When closing time came, they refused to buy.

I suggested to Darren he go into the next demo with no expectations. He was to do as he always did, but come closing, he wasn't to expect a sale. I told him to say the words, sincerely, but not to expect a positive response. Basically, he wasn't to worry about making the sale. The old saying, "You can't say the wrong thing to the right person," applies here.

To his credit, Darren took my advice to heart. In the following months, he bounced back to fifth in sales. His marriage woes dissipated and his income became steady again.

So now we have three lessons to work with, three powerful tools at your disposal to accelerate your activation.

They are:

1. Don't choose a path solely to make money. I'd made about $75,000 in eight months, but I was getting sick and felt miserable.

2. Find an experienced mentor that can give you want you need for success. No one else will do. They've put in the hours and developed a system that works. If they're willing to share that system (true mentors share), do your absolute best and don't waste their time—be direct about your objectives.

3. Expect nothing. In that, you'll find everything. With pressure removed, outcomes become favorable, big things happen. The idea of to just *chill* is key to help you let whatever is going to

> be…be. Don't be so eager. Trust that it will happen if it's supposed too. Keep your intentions pure and let the universe unfold its magic.

Your activity is to find a mentor. Find someone who can assist you with some aspect of your life. It doesn't have to be career related. It can be help with relationships, a hobby, or with your spirituality. Whatever your life needs, find a guide for it.

Being mentored will expedite your growth because I know you want things fast. If a mentor can help, find one. Or two.

What do you need, or want assistance with, from a mentor?

(ideas, goals, advice, further career, personal guidance, spiritual guidance, etc.)

6

Law of Manifestation

"We attract what we are ready for."

The story of my life has come to a point where I can introduce what I call the Law of Manifestation, or attraction. It's a force so powerful that science is still trying to understand its energy. You've all heard the saying, "What we think about, we bring about. Thoughts become things...." The premise is simple: where our thoughts go, reality follows.

You focus on bills and guess what you're always dealing with—bills. You focus on why a particular thing keeps happening to you, and it does! The Law of Manifestation can activate in an hour, a day, a year, or in my case, instantly.

Let me set the stage for one event—the grandest of productions. This one stimulated me to encourage you to embrace this law, or force. It now guides me through uncharted waters.

You might want to get really comfortable; this story is a doozy.

After I had finished selling Kirbys, my mother told me about a friend of hers that ran a string of fitness clubs in Irvine, California. If I wanted the job he was offering, it was mine. However, it was in southern California and I was on the central coast.

I met Scott, the owner, and we hit it off immediately. My gut said it would be a good growth opportunity as health and fitness was something that I was excited about. I put my house up for sale and headed south.

I found a small apartment right behind the club. Raquel, ready to leave her family again, left her job and joined me. Luckily, she was able to transfer to another hotel from the same chain where she currently worked. Everything seemed perfect—except my work hours.

I worked from seven in the morning to ten at night. My income was a commission job, so I had to be at work to earn. Being a good husband became a challenge since my life was mostly at the club. Don't get me wrong, I loved the opportunity and the promise of promotion. However, this was a tough job to enjoy. I constantly had to suck referrals from patrons in order to sign up new members. The business was all about numbers, and not by the week or month, but by the hour!

Now for the juicy part. I'm doing my best to spend time with Raquel, but I notice a disconnect. She frequently drove north with her new so-called friends (ones I'd never met). One night, waiting for her to return, it dawned on me that she would not. She wouldn't answer my calls, even after numerous attempts. I became concerned. But she did call, eventually, sounding disoriented.

She was up in Hermosa Beach with her friends, doing a photo shoot with some photographer and had fallen asleep. I asked her to return home. She said she would, but later. This was around six in the evening. She showed up at two in the morning.

The second she entered I felt an energy I'd never experienced. I began to ask her questions. "Where were you? Why didn't you call? What's really going on?" And one more: "Who is he?"

She denied anything improper, even after I pressed her. Finally, she said that I didn't know him. I literally collapsed to my knees, speechless. I had no clue what was going on, but I could see we were completely detached—she was so cold.

I took a day to try to figure it out. Was there a chance for us? But I could feel that her mind wasn't into staying together. So I asked her to be out of the apartment within three days. Her new friends drove in while I was at work and took her away. I never saw her again.

As you can imagine, this was a shock. I was devastated. But I managed to hold it together at work. However, word got out that I was single. Many of my coworkers, some women, offered to help me through my situation. I accepted. But mainly, I wanted to be left alone.

I decided to move in with my brother—he just happened to live nearby. My dog, Jordan, came too. I felt like we'd both been rescued. Then a series of events happened that could never be scripted for any movie, even if you tried.

A few days went by. Then, after returning from driving Jordan to the nearby dog park, I had just parked and opened my door when Jordan jumped out too quickly for me to stop him. There was a screech of brakes and a sickening cry from Jordan that I will never forget.

Jordan was trapped under the wheel of the vehicle. I had to tell the driver to reverse in order to free him. In tears, I drove him to a vet. They took him immediately and began to work on him. I stayed in the lobby, in distress too.

Jordan had a shattered hip and some internal trauma—still unchecked. The vets needed more time—48 hours—to find out what exactly he'd suffered. This would cost money, lots of it. My savings were rather meagre. On top of it all, Raquel had gone on a shopping spree. I was in debt.

I left the clinic an emotional wreck, teary-eyed, and generally in a bad place. At an intersection, my light red, I put my head down, crying, and said out loud, "All I need now is a car to hit me and this would truly be a bad day." As the last words left my mouth, there was a ear-shattering squeal of hard braking. The car to my left, stopped at the other signal, was hit by a white Shelby Mustang. It bounced off and came at me. My Toyota 4Runner was hit hard.

The impact rocked my car enough to break bones in my hand. The insurance company declared my car totaled. Thankfully, no one was seriously hurt. However, it was a sobering wake-up call. And, I'd become a living embodiment of this Law of Manifestation. Could the universe work that fast?

I'd gone from quite okay to rock-bottom in a week. I took some time off work. I needed to heal from the whiplash and bone fractures. With no job, I quickly found myself going broke—it wasn't possible to put in enough useful hours with an injured hand. In a month, with advice from an attorney friend, I filed for bankruptcy—Raquel had left me $20,000 in debt.

I wanted a clean slate. I wanted to remove all traces of Raquel from my life. I wanted a *new* life.

As time passed, I began to heal emotionally. Eventually, I found an amazing job at a private tennis club. I began as Director of Sales and Marketing. There were some great people to work with, most quite different than within the previous organization.

Working here, I regained my self-confidence. I made some really great friends and managed to get into the best physical shape of my life, playing tennis daily with members. They were upscale, professionals—a perfect spot for a hungry entrepreneur like myself. I stayed for two years, truly enjoying my time. But I missed being in a relationship.

I began applying the Law of Manifestation. Sure enough, one day a good friend called me from the airport saying that she had a vision of me wanting to meet someone special. And, she had a woman called Sara in mind. She gave me her number, telling me he had already told her about me. That was amazing. This Law of manifestation works pretty damned good! I called, not only because of my friend's advice, but also because my gut agreed.

Sara came to the tennis club one night. Immediately, we had a connection. She spoke the same language I did, was spiritual, affectionate, funny, and when she talked, looked you in the eyes. Her smile was huge, her demeanor spunky, energetic, and she dressed strikingly. In short, unique. I couldn't believe it—I'd found a female version of myself.

We became instant friends. She was an actor, did local theatre, and hung out with an eclectic tribe of fellow artists. I was accepted into this wonderful group. We married within a year.

At the time, this was the right thing to do. Looking back, we could have been just great friends. I enjoyed my time with her, but people evolve and life changes. Mine would. I'll get into more later.

Earlier, I introduced the concept of the Law of Manifestation, or attraction. Just to be clear, you don't have to be at rock-bottom to turn your life around. If you happen to be there now, you have the opportunity to change your life around instantly.

I learned that the more specific you are with your desires, the better the law works. But you must be ready, because when you do send out that energy, the response can be very subtle. However, it may hit you like a ton of bricks. In my case, a Shelby Mustang.

So, how do you apply this gift to your own life? Start by thinking about the things you desire. I know you don't want bad relationships, debts, student loans, lousy careers, etc. Concentrate on specific things that will improve your life. What kind of life-mate do you want? What kind of job and salary do you want? How much money would you like to have, and by when? Is your health a concern? Your family life? Be specific.

It's imperative that you get to the specifics of your desires. Nothing is out of reach. Dream big. Don't settle and don't make it easy—the universe loves serving people that know exactly what they want. You're one of the seven percent of humanity who will actually go through with this exercise, and do it many times a day.

Once you've made your list, the true magic begins. And you'll enjoy the fruits of your wishes.

Every morning, find a quiet place and spend a few moments reviewing your list. It only takes a few minutes. In a short time you'll see the desires that resonate with you. Spend some time with those and how they make you feel. See yourself meeting that perfect mate. Feel the emotion of owning a new home or moving to a more rewarding career. Imagine a bank balance that makes you smile.

I can tell you that this works. Once I understood this power, it changed my life forever. I've envisioned specific parking spaces at busy malls, thought about money showing up in my mailbox from something that happened long ago, and many things like that. I see myself with more energy every single day. That's why I'm a firecracker of energy.

There are two key elements you must understand:

1. You must create that list. Do it with emotion and feeling. It's not just a mechanical process; it must mean something.

2. You must see yourself, feel yourself, in that situation daily. Review your needs every morning and evening and enjoy the feeling it gives you.

This is your life you're creating. And you have more control over it than you've been telling yourself. I can personally assure you that if you're purposeful in these activities, your life will flourish. This is more than a once-a-week thing; this is an everyday thing. Remember, you're free to add to your list—the universe can handle it. It's waiting for you to challenge it. And once you've experienced what it can deliver, you'll get very excited and keep asking for more. Go ahead.

At the end of this book, I'll provide a way to keep your list organized and your desires honed to suit you best.

For now, create a list of ten things encompassing all aspects of your life that will be attractive to you for the next 90 days, or perhaps the next year. Be specific! Don't limit yourself. Have fun with it.

See yourself in possession of the desires on that list. The universe will do its part. Remember, focus on that list daily. Don't let it slip and become something you get to whenever.

Have fun, please. And make your life what you want it to be.

10 Things encompassing all aspects of your life that will be attractive to you for the next 90 days.

7

Mirror, Mirror on the Wall

"Get to know that person in the mirror. You'll be impressed."

Now that you've got a handle on the Law of Manifestation, keep using it—or else you'll fail to reap its rewards. With it, you'll have the ammunition to make a sizeable change to your life. Trust in yourself and the universe that changes will happen. Now, more on Sara.

An observation: After I returned home from work, toiling mostly by myself all day, having a conversation with my significant other felt like talking to myself again. It was sometimes a bit awkward. We were so alike that it felt like we were both on stage, performing. We both demanded the spotlight. There was no downtime. After a while, competing, we became distant.

We wanted different things, had different goals. As time went on, I needed an outlet to stir my creative juices. I needed to get into another groove and strove to refocus my energy using the Law of Manifestation. I wanted the universe to provide an opportunity, or an environment, to keep growing. Our relationship became strained.

Late one night, I somehow felt I needed to go to a bookstore. But it was after ten—nothing would be open. But….

My gut led me directly to the magazine rack. In the middle of hundreds of magazines, one cover had a picture of a white-haired man alongside a headline that read: *I Could Have Quit 6 Million Dollars Ago*. This man was "Ole" Paulie, and the magazine's focus was home businesses.

In Paulie's article, he described how he had helped many make money by working from home. At the end, they'd printed his phone number and email address. My gut said quickly, "Contact him." "Ole" Tony was going to do just that.

The next morning, I dialed and a friendly voice answered, saying, "I'm Ole Paulie." I was stunned. I was actually talking to the man who had this amazing story and had helped so many.

I told him, briefly, my story. Conversation with him was like talking to an old friend. He was a leader of a direct sales company, one that sold health and wellness products. And yes, he would work with me, as a mentor. Nothing about him seemed less than authentic. I was overjoyed.

He shipped me the book mentioned in the magazine article via overnight express. In it was an overview of the company's products. I signed up as a distributor that day.

Paulie turned out to be a very generous man. It's not hard to imagine that his success was a direct consequence of his willingness to help others. His life was rich in all aspects. He even flew me to meet him. Eventually, he became a father figure to me.

As such, he saw things in me that needed revealing: my teaching capability, my energy, my coaching ability. He decided I would be his next big project, and story.

Working with him was exciting, to say the least. He brought out my talents and let me shine onstage and in front of a room full of people. We had conversations about culture and building an army of followers simply by creating a culture that people would never want to leave. I knew he was a master at that. He would say, "Tony, if you create an environment where you build people's confidence, take time out to visit them, get to know them and their desires along with loving them, you'll be rich in all areas of your life." Wise words from a man who had built an empire with culture.

But there was more. Other things he taught me shaped me into the man I am today. You see, "Ole" Paulie was always willing to talk to people. His attitude was typically positive, upbeat. He saw good in everything. And he stressed that having control over your attitude is the one thing that everyone has. The altitude you fly in life is based on your attitude. Have a bad attitude, you'll have a distressing bank account. Have a good attitude, you'll like the balance in your account a lot more.

I've adapted this way of thinking for myself. My goal is to have the best attitude in the room. Paulie always wanted to make sure his attitude was an inspiration to others.

Yes, likely, he had bad days. His health, especially, gave him trouble. But you'd never know that. He was always king of the big "A."

Something else you should know. It's the reason I'm able to get so much done in the same 24 hours that everyone has. Paulie called it Sense of Urgency, or S.O.U.

Life's too short. Our most valuable commodity is time. What we end up doing with our time is our quality of life. If you sit on your butt and complain…well, enjoy that if you must. But you will not make that mistake, you'll spend your time wisely. Paulie didn't want to waste my time. Or his. He wanted to make sure that everything we did was in pursuit of something worthwhile, and to do it with a S.O.U. People are inspired by those who have an agenda (not to be interpreted here as a bad thing) and are on point. Overly long conversations about trivial matters wasn't his thing. Example: Do you really need two hours at the gym? Wouldn't one do? When you have a conversation, get straight to the point.

If you add S.O.U. to our day, my guess is that you'll find an extra six or seven hours of productivity and discovery. Mindless TV, reading the newspaper, are anathema to S.O.U. When you're on a mission, many things just don't matter.

Once you understand this principle, you'll get extra pep in your step. Read on, I'll show you how to embrace both S.O.U. and something I call "Chill Factor." But for now, you should focus on S.O.U. and implement just that. Remember, the universe loves you and loves speed. And you, you'll soon realize, have the need for speed in your blood too.

Over the years, Paulie and I would do many different things, business-wise. He loved selling books and tapes. Many times, I traveled the country in his company. I have many fond memories of our time together. He's responsible for many of the skills I now have. His influence is immense. And he came just at the time when I needed someone like him most.

This is what I learned:

1. Create a list of your talents, your skills, the things you're good at naturally, as well as your characteristics and attributes. Some things you know; some things your friends know better than you. Write them down.

   Your list might be quite long. Good. This is a very important list. It keeps you from focusing on your negative points. Create this list now.

2. What kind of culture have you created at home or with your friends? Is it a loving, welcoming, empowering culture? If not, it needs to be. What needs to be removed to improve this? What do you need to add? Remember, culture eats vision for lunch. Just for a moment, stand back and take stock. Do you want to be part of the culture you have created at work and at home?

3. Make sure you have the most positive attitude in the room. When you face the mirror, see how big a smile you can make. Make it hurt. Hold it for as long as you can. If you feel the need, pull your cheeks apart and hold them there.

   Focus on your energy and attitude. Check it hourly. Adjust it going into meetings, talking on the phone, when doing something you're not happy about. Use every opportunity to turn every moment into a positive one.

4. Why are you dragging your feet? Think S.O.U. Be that person that has the shorter conversation but gets more done and gets to the point sooner. Make today the day you light a fire under your butt. Be purposeful today. Now.

This should be a feel-good activity. I'll bet you didn't realize how wonderful a person you really are. It's time to celebrate this. Create that list, stretch that smile, get that sense of urgency. Create a masterpiece in yourself. You're going to love the finished product.

List your talents, skills, and what your closest friends would say are your best attributes:

How to GIVE Birth to a KONDOR

Cut out the ATTITUDE boxes below and tape them up on your mirror, fridge etc., so you see them all the time!

ATTITUDE

ATTITUDE

ATTITUDE

ATTITUDE

ATTITUDE

ATTITUDE

ATTITUDE

ATTITUDE

Cut out the S.O.U. boxes below and tape them up on your mirror, fridge etc., so you see them all the time!

S.O.U.

S.O.U.

S.O.U.

S.O.U.

S.O.U.

S.O.U.

S.O.U.

S.O.U.

8

Don't be a Twinkie

"Health is wealth."

I must congratulate you for pressing on and doing what I call the *good* and not the *work* in getting to this crucial chapter. Doing the work is not nearly as important as seeing what good the work brings to you.

Please, don't get the idea that this chapter is pushing my way of eating on you. I don't want to push anyone around. But I do want to show you how important diet is. To truly activate, to get to all the discoveries, you need to be healthy.

Good health is essential. It's a fact. You must honor the temple that is your body. That extends beyond what foods you eat to the environment you live in. So, in view of resting yourself, loving yourself, do the honorable thing by eating well and surrounding yourself with a positive environment.

Food is a major source of body pollution. Think alcohol, fast foods, sugar, starchy meals, and so much more. All this has gained America the unenviable reputation of having one of the unhealthiest populations in the world. Many go to seminars, read self-help books, hire life coaches, but fail to properly nourish their bodies. In effect, they're throwing their hard-earned money away. So what can we do?

Let me share more of my story. After an opportunity to work with a very successful business man arose in Chicago, I was asked to move from California to work with him. I wanted the move but Sara was adamant that she didn't want to be uprooted. I moved but she didn't.

I was given an ultimatum and chose, based on my gut, to move. It was the opportunity I had been manifesting. Sara said that if I moved, we would be done. We drifted apart and soon divorced.

You see, we were on different pages when it came to personal growth. We had outgrown the relationship. Change was upon me once again. Thankfully, the decision was mutual.

In Chicago, I began paying close attention to my eating habits. I began to eat cleaner. I no longer ate red meat. The occasional serving of chicken was okay. As a consequence, my energy level rose and my focus sharpened. The better I ate, the better I felt. My skin cleared up and I slept better—the change upon me was very enjoyable. I got excited about becoming knowledgeable about the best foods for my body. Certainly, I benefited greatly.

Because of that, I'm now an advocate of proper eating and giving your body the fuel it needs to perform at optimum. As humans, most of us *know* what's good for us. However, an occasional special meal or rich dessert is fine. But be careful not to get lost in its addictive appeal—don't treat each meal as your last one.

The result of organic eating, staying relatively sugar-free, refusing processed foods, staying away from food fillers, pesticides and chemicals, is life-changing in more ways than one. "You are what you eat."

So true.

The lesson I learned was to eat as organically as possible. When food shopping, stay away from the aisles—that middle section. The grocery store perimeter is your friend. Green and colorful produce is always good. You can never eat enough fruits and vegetables, adding some nuts for energy. Keep your home well stocked with these.

I'm over 50 years old, but I have lots of energy. My body craves good, healthy food. In time, yours will too. Your smartphone app store will have healthy recipe cookbooks. Once you remove the heavy foods, meats and sugars from your diet, your taste buds will come alive.

At 43, I cut out all meats except fish and drastically reduced my dairy intake. My health improved dramatically.

Later in the book, I'll outline another major change I made in my lifestyle with the aim of improving my vitality.

To begin this process for yourself, reduce the amount of sugar you consume. Educate yourself on the ingredients in foods so you can make informed choices.

The media is full of great documentaries on better eating. And, of course, the internet is your friend.

What does your gut tell you to eat? What does your body temple need at this moment? These are good questions. Find the right answers.

Your brain will want Rice Krispies, cheesecake, pizza, and chocolate. Don't listen to it. Your body temple is the only one you have. It loves foods rich in nutrients, not rich foods. The result, clarity like you've never experienced.

With that in mind, let's go on to the following exercise:

- Go through your cupboards and pantry. Read ingredient labels. Find those foods that have high sugar (this includes fructose), high sodium (salt), or those that are simply over-processed and unhealthy—this is your opportunity to feel liberation at a whole new level—and toss them.

Raid your refrigerator and do the same. The inside of your refrigerator should be alive with the colors of nature.

The first time I did this, I truly felt like I was in control. I cranked the radio volume and began reading labels. I did a happy dance to the trash every time I found something I never wanted to eat again. I would no longer weaken my immune system with chemicals, processed sugars and preservatives.

By now, you're on an amazing journey. You need energy without guilt. You need that sharpened focus. Clean those cupboards and brush up on nutrition. There's power in education.

Cheers to your health !

9

Growth is Good

"Discovery is the first step to mastery."

Personal development is a lifelong process. At different stages in life, we embrace the idea of growing to another level. I like the word "discover" better. When my life was manifesting wonderful things, I was deep into discovery.

To help quench my thirst for information, I engaged my teachers, bought CDs, attended different health events. When my path veered away, I'd get lost in a dark alley asking anyone for directions to get back on a steady roadway. Many times I asked the wrong person and got steered the wrong way.

When I said goodbye to Sara, we agreed that we simply outgrew the relationship. Remember, we know change is good, often welcome. Sara was a wonderful teacher. To this day, I admire her zest for life and her ability to find beauty in everything. In that, we are so alike.

In Chicago, I changed my eating habits—my personal growth was once again on the rise. The environment I found myself in was conducive to growth, the people talk the talk and walk the walk. I grew more and manifested more. I focused on my goals, discovered more daily, and realized how fast the universe works.

Let me give you one huge piece of advice, one which you should write down: acts, whether physical or mental, if done consistently (every day, no exceptions), will always bear fruit. The key word here is *consistently.*

Consistently exercise and you'll reach your goals. Consistently eat well and your health will improve. Think consistently and you'll get the answers you need. The key: be consistent.

At this stage of my life, I met someone who would turn out to be the most dynamic representation of love I would ever meet.

Remember, I can only manifest that of which I am. A person will only attract what they are at that moment. It's true, believe me.

When you were single, all your friends were single. When you had a boy or girlfriend, you had friends that were dating. If you've ever been married, all your friends were couples. If you have kids, all your friends were dysfunctional, just like you. I say dysfunctional because I have a teenager now. Apparently, in his eyes, I'm the dysfunctional one. In effect, your environment is a byproduct of you at this moment. Growing affects that.

So, more of my story.

With all this growth, I noticed my finances had improved, I enjoyed better health, had more energy, was more to the point, and I loved myself.

I'd been through a lot in the last fifteen years: marriages, bankruptcy, an accident, loss of employment, and a severely bruised ego. And, occasionally, that horror movie starring George played nonstop in my head.

But I had turned my life around utilizing my gut for guidance and a willingness to embrace change combined with a never-surrender attitude.

So, by the time I met Rhonda, I was in a high-growth period and loving myself for who I was. I had conquered quite a lot. While speaking at a motivational event, I met her and some of her girlfriends. She introduced herself, saying how she enjoyed my talk and felt inspired by it. We continued with small talk and parted. A few months later, at another event, we met again in the lobby of the hotel. From there, everything started to go at Mach 10.

After the night's live band festivities, we sat in the hotel lobby and began talking. We talked about life, business, family, future, goals, aspirations and so many other things. Deep conversations. Simple conversations. We talked, talked, talked and talked. My S.O.U. (Sense of Urgency, remember?) at that time was nonexistent. But I wanted to savor every moment with her. And my attitude was the best it had ever been.

This woman fascinated me. In her presence, a calm came over me like never before. I felt I already knew her and we would live happily ever after. If manifestation was to present its power, now was the time!

We continued talking when all of a sudden we noticed people we knew walk by asking us to join them for breakfast. We had spent the whole night sitting on the lobby sofa talking. Much time had slipped by. I knew she was going to steal my heart.

We stayed in touch, her in Lincoln, Nebraska, and me back in Chicago. Thank goodness for an unlimited calling phone plan because Rhonda and I talked 15 to 20 times a day. Over the phone, we developed a deep relationship.

This long-distance love affair continued for a few months. Then I got the call that she was coming to Chicago—to be with me. My attitude was off the charts. We bought a house together, lived in Chicago for a year, got married, and when my work was done there, I asked her if she wanted to move back home to Lincoln.

In Lincoln we decided to have a child. Something I thought I never wanted. But one day, she said, "You don't know what love is until you have your own child." She already had two wonderful kids. Apparently, since she's the goddess of love, she knows what she's talking about.

We owned a couple of daycare centers in Lincoln and I spent most of my time managing that business and doing sales. Those kept me from having to be with the children twelve hours a day. Rhonda and I realized that we also loved direct sales. To that end, we found a company to join and start promoting.

I understand the power of residual income and wanted to build a legacy. The company was big on personal health *and* even bigger on personal growth.

This type of company was perfect for me. It served two of my needs: the need for growth and the need to serve others. It was at this time that I found one of my passions: the more I help others, the more I help myself.

I truly love to help others. I love to read books about leadership and accounts of people who just went for it despite the odds.

From birth, you're growing. Your brain expands, your muscles and organs strengthen and your spirit is ready to soar. Growth is vital. And knowledge is power; education is wisdom. Let growth be the fuel that runs your life. Don't let it die on the vine. Don't say, "That's it." Say, "What's next?" or "What else do I do to grow?"

During this growth period, I learned a very important lesson on how to stay ahead of the game and live a life that offers others inspiration. It's called taking out the trash.

The concept of getting rid of things that negatively affect your life is liberating. I said goodbye to news, television, social media (to a degree), certain people, and jobs and situations that no longer served me well.

All too often, we tend to cling to things that make us uncomfortable. I don't know where that gene comes from, but we need to both acknowledge it exists and get rid of it. In all my readings, it's obvious that it's an absolute truth that our close circle consists of, in effect, no more than five friends. We need to choose those five with great care.

So, do you rid yourself of someone who's been a buddy since childhood? If he's a negative influence, yes. Maybe, upon reflection, you realize he's been miserable, a complainer, and has been that way forever.

This is not to say you can't have more than five friends. But be aware of the five you spend most of your time with. Are they serving a menu that consists of empowerment, growth, stimulation and opportunity? If not, reconsider their prominent placing. Rid yourself of the soothsayers, negative Nellies, anyone that's not assisting you to move forward.

You must, absolutely, take out the trash. Don't disown them, just don't buy into their drama. This is vital. Get your power back. Find a new circle of five. Demote or remove anyone that's negative. You can't grow a rose in the mud. Your goal is to find your five. If you only have one right now, that's fine, but stay alert for the next and the next.

Letting go is cleansing. It's necessary for advancement. I hear you, thinking in your heart that I'm right. If so, do what needs to be done. Don't frequent anyone who beats you down. A friend must be positive and rewarding. With those, you'll grow. And so will they.

Your passion to grow is your lesson. When you grow, you exist. Read daily, take out the trash, pay close attention and protect your personal environment. This will give you power beyond imagination.

These are your action steps for this chapter:

1. Read 15 to 30 pages daily. The subject can be autobiography, leadership, spiritual life, anything that contains inspirational words. Remember, consistency is the key. Develop a passion for knowledge and expand your intelligence. There's power and stability in knowledge.

2. Take out the trash. Think hard about what surrounds you in your office, your home, and in your closet. Clothes you don't wear, the junk—get rid of it. Bag it and give to it to charity or the

homeless. Spend a day, collect it all and just do it. This could be the feel-good act you've been really needing. Bless someone with your castoffs—they'll be grateful.

3. Protect your personal environment. Imagine living in a bubble filled with positivity, prosperity and unlimited growth. Remove those things that don't support this and people that aren't of that genetic makeup.

It's time to clean house on social media, friends and family that...well, you get it. If you must, consider moving or changing employer or career.

I can't even guess at the number of jobs, cars, friends, homes, and fashion changes I've gone through. Each time something gets removed, something wonderful comes to replace it or something magical happens. You have to let the past go to grow. Remember, change is good. A new, clean environment just may make your spirits soar.

Later in this book, I'll go into more detail into the action steps to protect your environment and how it's possible to grow in three different life-enriching bubbles.

What is the next book you are going to read?

Commit to 15 to 30 minutes a day—set an alarm or calendar reminder if you have to. Be consistent!

Title of the book you are going to read:

What are the items that no longer serve you ?

Clothing, jewelry, shoes, accessories etc., are all items you can give to others. They will appreciate them.

Write down the first things that you're going to get rid of:

Protect your environment!

Who do you need to stop interacting with?

What habit(s) do you need to change or stop?

What do you need to add or change in your environment?

What kind of people do you want to surround you?

10

I was Runnnnninggg!

"In your moment of darkness, you will see your light."

This is a bonus chapter, dedicated to one of my most interesting challenges. As I've said before, I love health and fitness. And I love to challenge myself.

I've jumped from airplanes, climbed mountains, learned an entire album of music from a band called Farewell 2 Fear (in which I now play full-time) in order to perform in front of thousands, swam with stingrays, became a world-class comedy stage hypnotist, and even had a son.

One day, however, I was thinking what the ultimate challenge would look like. What do I dislike most and makes no sense to me? Looking at it that way, the answer came quickly. I despise running, and marathons are the most ludicrous thing the body can endure. So that was my challenge: running a marathon.

I searched online for the next marathon and found it would be the LA Marathon, less than 90 days away. This race is the third largest in the country. Over 30,000 people race 26.2 miles. Why would so many do this?

This would be the ultimate test of preparation, mental toughness, physical stress and navigating the unknown. Certainly a challenge for me.

I hate running. Nevertheless, I entered and began my research on how to prepare to run this daunting thing. Running that long when you hate running is downright stupid, on my part. In my research, I found one gentleman that had run over 100 marathons. I figured this man *must* know how.

Remember, I like to go straight to the source of knowledge. He'd be the perfect mentor. I downloaded his blueprint for training. The schedule it contained was one year in length. I had 89 days and counting. Time for S.O.U.! And time to tap into my special powers and get working.

I'm not subject to Obsessive Compulsive Disorder (OCD), but seeing how some have died training for, or running in, marathons, they must have been more than driven to push so hard.

I had a negative attitude going in. I hated the thought of running (I know, I've said this before) the 26.2188 miles (to be exact). It's not a normal thing to subject a body to. I would rather drive that distance in comfort, enjoying radio and air conditioning. Nevertheless, I resolved to do whatever my cheat sheet asked me to do—no shortcuts, no excuses, no wimping out.

I dreaded the days I had to run. Day one, I went 2 miles. Day three, after a day of rest, 5 miles—every step painful. I asked myself, is this really necessary? But I don't quit. I knew, inside, I *had* to do this and quickly changed from *stinkin thinkin* to *atta boy*.

After the first week, my body actually got more comfortable with the running. Somewhat. I drank tons of water, took salt tablets, and ate more than I ever did. But I adjusted.

After the second week, I could manage 15 miles. Not bad. And I *was* actually getting comfortable running. I studied about running shoes, special running socks, and the right foods to fuel the body after extended periods of stress. This new knowledge excited me. And, for the first time, I was a bona fide runner.

I bought the right clothing, a heart rate monitor, those special socks, moisture wicking underwear, Band-Aids to protect my nipples (really?) and a fanny pack to store snacks.

The Band-Aids, I read, were needed because sweat-drenched shirts rub sensitive skin raw. This actually happened to me. I've never felt anything so painful. Anyway, back on course.

My base run was now to run 25 miles for a week. I'd become a real runner, for sure. And I felt really, really good. My doubts about finishing faded and my competitive nature kicked in.

My first goal was to actually finish without dire consequences—like death! But I wasn't quite ready to give my family my life insurance just yet. I decided the way to improve was to give myself goals along the way.

My sister, who'd run a few marathons, suggested anything under 6 hours was a respectable finish time. Her best time was 5:45. I wanted to best that. But my first goal was to survive the race.

My second was to finish under 5:45, preferably around 5 hours. Breaking the 4-hour mark made no sense for me.

I continued to train. A week before race day, I ran 22 miles. Just before the race, I'd run shorter distances so as not to get too tired on the day of the race.

It was a rather crazy thing that I had built up to that level of competency. Still, after those 22 miles, could I have run another 4.2? Runners describe a thing called a runner's high. I never experienced that. It was always pure work.

On race day I made a discovery. I'll never forget it. You won't either. After eating my by-the-book breakfast, drinking the by-the-book water, I headed for Dodger Stadium. I had all my gear and knew the pace I had to run to be competitive.

If I felt like a superhero, I would try for a sub 4-hour run. I laugh about this now, still. That goal didn't make sense.

Anyway, I got into it, knew at what mile I'd be eating, drinking, taking salt tablets. OCD sufferers are great planners. I was a great planner. Did I have OCD?

In the middle of those 30,000 racers at the starting gate, I was overwhelmed. We were all bunched together. Then the gun went off.

For the first quarter mile, I was simply shuffling my feet, attempting to break free, going nowhere. It was a race, for goodness sakes—let's go people! Finally, I settled into my stride and felt very strong as the adrenaline pumped through my veins.

I saw my family at mile 8. We'd planned this. But when I came over the hill, hearing my wife and son screaming my name, emotion got the better of me. I burst into tears, swallowed in their love and support. It was a magical moment.

I kept running, my muscles, finely tuned as they were, doing their job as my head dissolved. I had to continue, not break stride. I didn't want to cramp up or tighten; that would slow me down. I knew this from my research. I love being knowledgeable. Knowledge is power.

Here's where the lessons I learned came. Around mile 13, I witnessed what happened to those not fully prepared. Some walked, some coughed, many were not enjoying this one bit.

At mile 18, I remember going up a hill just before descending downtown towards Rodeo Drive when a sight I could not fully explain confronted me. A group of people surrounded a man, flat on his back, giving him CPR. To my left, another guy did a number 2 on the sidewalk. Some others urinated. Some puked. In all, quite surreal.

Those were the ones not prepared. A race this challenging needs full preparation. As in life, be prepared. Then my head started up, telling me I'd be next.

Was *I* adequately prepared? I began to doubt my training. Crazy how the mind wants to sabotage. But I knew I was ready. I shook off the negative thoughts.

My training was textbook. I was in the best shape of my life. I had this. My gut agreed. I quickly focused and continued.

And more encouraging, I was ahead of the 5-hour time. A second wind kicked in.

I picked up the pace and ran with more pep in my stride. I was feeling good despite the tricks my mind had conjured. I found myself with a clear head again. Then it happened.

While running a marathon, there's usually a sign, a banner that you run under, with the mile count. When I got to mile 25, I didn't know if I had just completed 25 or if I was beginning the 25th. I'd completely lost track of where I was. I looked at my watch and felt I could break the 4-hour barrier. But, was I behind? So I did the only thing that made any sense—run as fast as I possibly could, for as long as I could.

I took off at a full sprint. In the distance, I could hear the cheers from the crowd at the finish line. I still had a long way to go. But I kept my pace. Maybe I would go under 4 hours. As I got closer, I felt a peace come over me. At the finish, the clock read 4:11. I had finished! And done very well. But where was my family?

I noticed my watch time was faster than the official clock. Still, I couldn't find my family. But there was lots of people there, all waiting for their runner. I kept searching, then pondered the time discrepancy.

I wandered over to the timekeeper's tent and asked. They took my race number and said they'd check. By that time, 30 minutes had elapsed and still my family wasn't anywhere to be found. I wanted to celebrate with them. Apparently, they didn't think I'd finish so quickly.

Back at the timekeeper. 3:59:28! I had finished in less than 4 hours! More tears. I had dedicated so much time to training and pushed myself like never before—and it had paid off.

This was the ultimate test for me and I'm proud to say that in the history of marathons, you're reading a book from a guy that's in the top quarter of people that run marathons. Only 25% that finish a marathon do it in less than 4 hours. I'm world class, baby.

Today, my running days are over, but this brief period in my life taught me so many lessons.

Here they are for you:

1. We must challenge ourselves. Challenges help us discover who we really are. What challenge are you willing to accept that will *truly* test your essence?

2. Educate yourself in the things that interest you. Knowing the good, bad, and ugly about marathon running made me mentally stronger. I was prepared. Doing research, finding a mentor, were crucial to my success.

3. Put in the miles; prepare yourself. I did everything by the book. I ran the race contained in the script. I trusted the wisdom of others and trusted that my body, mind, and spirit would strengthen after I trusted the process. Those not prepared fell by the wayside. It's the same in life. Prepare, put in the miles.

4. Just go. Near the end of the race, when I sprinted, I pushed myself. When I thought I could go no harder, I went harder. I discovered there's always a bit more to squeeze out. Don't say to yourself, "This is it." My heart pushed my head aside and I finished the race strong. We all have heart. Use it!

The activity you choose must be something that's going to push you to discover who you are. What endeavor will test your physical and mental being? What will test your heart?

If it's a foot race, I applaud you. If you give that race your very best, euphoria is right around the corner. Just watch for mile 18—it'll give you nightmares. Life is a marathon with a series of sprints. Pace yourself!

Choose your challenge and share it with me.

My challenge is:

Date of challenge:

Why I am doing my challenge:

How to GIVE Birth to a KONDOR

My mentor or accountability partner is:

____

____

Two final action items for you:

1. Document, on all your social media channels, the journey of your challenge with pictures and videos to inspire others.
2. Send me an email, at kondorsociety@gmail.com, when you have completed your challenge and tell how it has impacted you and what it has meant to you.

☐ Email sent ______________________

11

It's Alive

"We are all capable of so much more."

Marriage to Rhonda taught me so much. As I've mentioned, she's the yin of my yang. We complement each other in powerful ways.

After we'd been together for a year and had planned our wedding, she told me that I wouldn't know real, deep love until I'd had a child of my own. She had two children from her prior marriage. But I thought, "No, I'm fine like I am now." I didn't need more responsibility. Plus, being a stepdad was difficult enough. Those that are stepparents know exactly what I am talking about.

Then one day we were just relaxing and our small talk turned into a big-boy, big-girl conversation.

Rhonda said, "I'm not getting any younger. If I ever want another child, it has to be now. My biological clock is ticking. Now is the best time to experience a deeper meaning of love."

My own child? Was I ready? The more I thought about it, the more my heart said, "Yes." I wanted to be the kind of father I never had, and I wanted to continue my name and be a dad. We held each other and well…went to work.

One of the things I wanted was to be kept in the dark about the sex of our unborn baby. For nine months, I called our baby "It." I believe there are too few true surprises. Knowing your child's sex early ruins the excitement. Those who've waited know this. It's kind of like opening a Christmas gift before the big day. On Christmas Day, you go, "Well, that's nice," and hope it sounds authentic.

I would rub Rhonda's tummy and say, "I love you, It. All I want for you is to be healthy." What she didn't hear me say is, "But I want you to have a penis like your daddy!"

Nine months later, our It was born. I videotaped the birth. It was obvious that this event could never, ever be repeated. It was then that my life's purpose became clear to me.

I had a new baby boy with the woman I cherished. Between us, we had to take good care of this child. I would do whatever it took to honor his presence in my life. He was the true meaning of love.

For the first nine hours, he didn't have a name. I wanted him to have a special name, one that encompassed his complexion, shape and personality. Nurses would come in and ask what name we'd chosen. I would say, jokingly, "Name? We don't even know who the father is!" That got a laugh from the nurses but a grimace from Rhonda.

Then, in a moment of solitude, I looked down at him and saw the innocence of this gift. His eyes met mine and I knew he should be a Tony.

He would be my one and only child, the truest representation of love one can experience. Every responsibility I undertook would focus on this child. Rhonda was already a pro mom; she understood what came next.

All this so I can introduce the word *love*. It's the most powerful word in any language. What people do in its name is unfathomable.

Love does conquer all. Love moves mountains. Love is all there is.

Your quest is to find love. Do love. Discover love. Share love. Be loved. Cherish love. Promote love. Embrace love.

Open yourself to love. Be open to love. Experience love everywhere. Love finds a way, love heals, love prevails. Oh, and finally, start with loving that person you see in the mirror. When you love yourself, you can truly love others.

I love you.

12

The Call

"Tears cleanse the soul."

I mentioned earlier that my stepbrother, George's son, was to live with him. After all, George was his father. He felt that he should raise his own son.

Mom had a difficult time with this. She felt guilty abandoning him. But George was adamant. It was his way or no way.

So, George Jr. grew up with his father. The way George ruled the house was all the boy understood. As he got older, the pressure to perform at 100 percent all the time became unrealistic. Junior quickly became a man.

Junior, enduring the same environment as I had, developed his own superpowers in order to cope. He excelled at sports and was popular with girls. He was a good looking kid with the mental strength of a general—an all-American boy.

He was a star football player; his jersey number: 54. Everyone loved him. Basically, he was a cool kid. In high school, he discovered his identity, as young men do. Then, one night, everything changed—his girlfriend was pregnant.

Even at 37, when my son was born, it was a ton of responsibility. George Jr. survived it a while. But one weekend, it all came to a grinding halt. On his way home, alone in his truck, his father out of town, he decided to take his own life.

The pressure, the guilt, the prospect of facing his father, was too much. Coming off the highway, instead of slowing, he sped up and crashed through the guardrail and into a tree. They found alcohol. The truck was totaled. Junior suffered massive lacerations and broken bones. The outcome was grim.

He managed to survive, but was heavily medicated for pain. Somehow, he was able to call his best buddy and convince him to help him escape. Between them, they left the hospital.

Junior sent his buddy home, convincing him that he just needed rest. Finally alone, he planned his next move as he hadn't finished what he'd set out to do. He wrote a note, found his father's gun and followed through.

Mom called, hysterical. "Tony, Junior. Shots, neighbor, driveway, Junior, dead, two shots. Tony, Junior is dead." I couldn't believe my ears. It made no sense. But it did sink in—Junior had taken his life, succeeding on the second try in 24 hours.

That tragic event affected our family for a long time. It was my darkest moment. But I discovered a light.

His funeral changed my life. I'd never had anyone this close to me move on before. Hundreds of kids showed up to see him off, to honor him. He was loved and admired, a gift to the world for the short time he graced it.

As a family, we tried to keep it together. When I met Mom in the parking lot, she wanted to show me something. She walked me over to the car, pointed out a bag of 54 balloons that we would release at the cemetery. When she opened the door, one balloon escaped, floating up to heaven. We stared at each other. She thought they were all secured in the trash bag.

Obviously, Junior did not want to be in there. So he fled. Mom and I hugged as we watched Junior float away. Inside, we shared the escape with my siblings. They smiled, connected, and the ceremony began.

During the reading of the Eulogy, the lights suddenly flickered. Literally, they went off then on again—quite a few times. It was as if someone was playing with the light switch. But who'd do that? So disrespectful. Was it Junior?

After five minutes of this, everyone distracted, my family broke into smiles. Junior was having his fun. Growing up, he was the ultimate prankster. He was at it again.

Then, from outside, the sound of car alarms. First one, then more. Our smiles turned into laughter. Junior wasn't going to let up. He was here with us, letting us know he was finally happy.

The ceremony completed, his best friends escorted the casket as it was loaded into the hearse. Then we got into our cars for the drive to the cemetery. Our family was first in line but we just sat there waiting. For what? For ten minutes we just stayed put. What was going on? Why not just go? Then this guy comes running with jumper cables. Another car pulls up next to the hearse, hoods open, and they attempt to jump-start it.

Junior was in control. Had I tried, I could not have come up with this series of events. During this time, I discovered and felt the power of spirit.

I don't know what you believe in, but I know now, without a shadow of a doubt, that energies, spirits, angels, frequencies and vibrations, when you're in tune and awake, are present. You cannot deny it.

Have you ever felt a presence? Have you ever been attracted to an object, symbol or number, that keeps reappearing? In my case, it's the number 54.

When I'm on the right track, I see this number in movies, on my phone in the form of battery percentage, or time. It's my guardian Junior letting me know that all is well and I'm on the right track.

Your activity is to identify anything that's happened to you that is unexplainable. Tap into that event. Be open to it. Honor and accept it.

Your body emits so much energy you just have to believe that magic and miracles are possible. We can be guided if we allow it to happen and remain open to the possibilities of a higher energy.

I'll share another experience at the end of the book showing that there are other levels, other dimensions, that we have yet to tap into.

Are there signs or feelings that make sense to you? Do you feel the presence of a guide, one that's looking out for you?

Is this too deep for you? Get ready, later, we're going deep together. But no need to worry, I've done all the hard work. You'll just be asked to enjoy the ride.

Write down any thoughts or feelings you have about being guided. Are any event inexplicable? What was happening at the time? Did this feeling reoccur? Write them down and acknowledge them here:

13

It's a Question of Love

"An open heart has the ability to open a closed door."

We've done some heavy lifting, especially in the last chapter. However, I want you to know that I love all the beautiful work you've done.

Designing a life is not easy. Most of us have never been taught how. But we're more fortunate than most—we have this book to guide us. And remember, the sequence, or timeline, outlined in this book is designed to give you immediate and permanent results.

Next, I'll cover a topic I know you'll thoroughly enjoy. Included is an introduction to an intelligent old friend, one that's been patiently waiting in the background yet in many ways has always had the limelight. I'm referring to your heart.

Your brain, strong and smart, has the ability to be the loudest voice in your body. It's always thinking, telling you you're hungry, you have a headache, you need this and that. Its thoughts go on and on, nonstop. All the while, your heart is quietly keeping you alive just waiting to be activated.

Your heart should be your guide, not your brain. It's like your own PhD of life. Your gut was your Master's Degree, needed to understand life. But now that you need to grow, you should listen to your heart, especially during quiet times.

For ten years, after years of study, I was a comedy stage hypnotist. I understand the power of the mind and how it works. Literally, it's our computer. It processes, stores and executes. But it likes to play games too. It also creates stories, doubt and fear.

Most of us are governed by the thoughts that our brains produce. This makes us vulnerable to a disease that's killed more people than any other: the "Yeah But" disease.

When we get a great idea to do something we know we should be doing or get that feeling that we just must do something, the brain suddenly jumps in and says, "Yeah but, you've tried that before. What are your friends going to think? You don't have time for that. You don't know anything about that. It's impossible. Blah, blah, blah." It paralyzes you. How many times has this happened?

However, there is a vaccine for this disease. And, to allay your fears, you'll actually enjoy the cure—no prickly needles necessary.

All that's needed is some quiet time during which you can tune into yourself. Simply sitting still for a few minutes is great therapy. I've used the word *meditation* a few times, so let's go down that path again.

Meditation is one of my main tools—I call it Tony time. It's the time I set aside, morning, afternoon and evening, to reconnect with myself. I don't have a set time to do this, but I can tell you that it's part of my daily routine.

If you really think about it, your heart is your body's hardest working organ. It's constantly in motion, constantly pumping blood and oxygen through the thousands of miles of vessels every second of your life. It pumps more when you need it, less when you don't. It does exactly what your body needs. Meditation, or quiet time, allows you to check in, appreciate and listen to your heart.

The benefits of meditation number in the hundreds: reduced headaches, blood pressure, and stress; more spiritual and physical energy; better relaxation, focus and balance; more awareness, and so many more.

Earlier, I talked about listening to your gut. Now it's time to focus on your heart. Myself, I simply follow its lead.

My heart goes deeper than my gut. I often ask the question, "What does my heart want to do right now?" Immediately, I take notice of the feeling that my mind processes and change that into an action. Every time, it's been the right thing to do.

I'll go into how to meditate at the end of the book—I'll show you how to turn 18 minutes into a very effective meditative base.

Even when you're in line at a checkout, you can drift into a state of quietness and check in with your heart. Take a few deep breaths and ask, "What do you want? What do you need me to do right now?" Then turn into an action the first answer it gives you.

The more you go straight to the source—bypassing your mind—the more dynamic the feeling will become. Your heart muscle is always available, always ready to serve you. You already know it will fulfill your physical needs. Now you know it will give you mental clarity as well.

Here's a simple feel-good exercise that will activate this mental strength. Take your right hand and place it on your chest. Say aloud, "What do you want me to do?" The first feeling you get is your answer.

To make this even more powerful, close your eyes, take a deep breath—hold for four seconds—and ask your heart again. Then exhale. Doesn't that feel great!

You can use this technique as often as you wish. Your heart muscle is the strongest one you own; you won't be able to ask too much from it. Your heart is life.

The quality of your life is based on the amount of love and connection you have with your heart. Remember, always ask for direction, answers and strength, from within. Your gut will protect you and your heart will guide you—quite a one-two combination!

Now, if you ask your heart what to do next, what are the chances that it will tell you to move on to the next chapter?

See you there.

14

Set Me Free

"Let it go so you can grow."

This chapter might be a bit uncomfortable. Earlier, I mentioned the concept of taking out the trash. That is, removing the clutter and making the needed adjustments to your environment. In effect, protecting it.

I also said quite a bit about my stepfather, George. As you know, living with him was sometimes unpleasant. And then there's the other difficult moments: being teased, friends stabbing me in the back, my business going under, those I trusted taking my money and fleeing. My life has been a series of relationships and events that created havoc with my daily routine.

Besides using my superpowers—which I now use most days—what was it about all those awful things that pushed me farther forward than anything else? Forgiveness.

Forgiveness just might be all that's left when all is said and done with our time together. And the lack of forgiveness is often the only thing holding us back.

So let's spend a few moments reviewing an event that forced me headlong into the concept of forgiveness.

Through Rhonda's mother, we met a wonderful woman who offered a unique approach to identifying and dealing with the chatter that fills our heads and governs our lives. This woman conducted a week-long seminar that helped me understand the power of forgiveness.

A few days into the seminar, we had to write about an event in our own lives that we had to let go of. The idea was to face and deal with that event, and let it go in our own way. It was during this process that I came face to face with George in a very vibrant and detailed vision.

I saw him walking from a white light, coming to face me directly. His hair had gone white but he was still that broad and strong man. He wore awful plaid pants, a white shirt and a beige coat. He smiled at me. In my mind, I heard him say, "I'm sorry." For this man to utter those words…I can't imagine how hard that was for him.

Granted, it was only a vision, but it felt as real as anything I have felt in his presence. He went on to tell me that he didn't know how to love me. His father had not treated him very well. And though he wanted to do better, it was uncomfortable for him. He loved us in his own way, truly, but was simply unable to bring himself to say it aloud or show it physically.

Again, he said, "I'm sorry." Then he added, "I'm asking for your forgiveness. Will you forgive me?" He put his head in my lap and cried.

I told him that I loved him for being the single most influential person in my life. Because of him, I strove to become a good person.

I also wanted to show him I was a strong person—once a kid and now a man. He, in his own authoritative way, made me resilient. Under his rule, I became a superhero. I said, "I forgive you." He hugged me and walked back into the light.

I understood the power of forgiveness. I was, in effect, cleansed. I also knew that the angel that came to me bearing George's form was cleansed too. Forgiveness heals all wounds.

Because of George, I carried many wounds. But in this moment, they all healed. I was able to let go and let be. I felt lighter, my face softer, and my heart beat freer. That was forgiveness.

It was also then that I felt forgiveness of self. I had to forgive myself for all the evil thoughts and words that I'd said about him. There were times I wanted him to die—just go and die. That's terrible. A kid shouldn't be thinking those things. I had to forgive myself for all the hurt I might have inflicted on him during my childhood. Knowing the true power of manifestation, I'm sure I hurt him. My thoughts and energies must have had a negative effect on him—and probably fueled his anger.

In all, I learned to forgive so I could truly live.

A few months later, I got a call from my mother. George had passed away. The funeral was to be in California, where he lived. My heart told me to go and say goodbye.

After greeting my brother and sister, I walked over to the open casket. I didn't tear up, felt no heart flutters. I was simply at peace.

He wore the exact same outfit I saw in my vision. I smiled and told him that I loved him and thanked him for molding me into the man I am today. I leaned down and whispered, "I forgive you." I forgave myself and asked that he forgive me for any hurt or harm I might have caused.

My heart had been full since that day. I could let go and grow.

George spent the last five years of his life battling a horrible disease. That alone was enough for a man to endure. I wanted him to know that I loved him and forgave him.

So now we turn back to ourselves. My friends, who in your life, including yourself, do you need to forgive?

The act of forgiveness, with the right intent, will remove the shackles that keep you prisoner. There are two ways to go about this.

One, do it physically. Make the connection in person and be the one that takes the high road and says that regardless of what has happened, I'm in a better place and I forgive you for ______________________________. Fill in the space.

The second is through a letter. A physical letter—in your handwriting. It doesn't have to be long, but it does have to be in your words. Don't use email; it's too easy to misinterpret. Finally, use prayer or quiet time to reflect.

I realize some situations cannot be addressed head on. For these, in your quiet time, you can acknowledge the situation, offer forgiveness and let the energy and frequency you release do its work.

Regardless, flip the switch, turn the corner and change your life so you're comfortable with the act of forgiveness. Begin cleansing.

Who, right at this moment, do you need to forgive? Don't forget yourself. I'll forgive you for almost forgetting that one—but it's the most important.

I'm so grateful I got to share this part of my life with you. The next half of the book is going to transport you to a far more interesting place.

Take a few deep breaths and prepare yourself—but after you do this exercise: write down the name, or names, of those you know in your heart you must forgive.

Now, doesn't that feel good?

Who or what do you need to forgive ?

What is/are their name(s)?:

Describe the situation:

How will you forgive them?

- ☐ Face to face
- ☐ By handwritten letter

15

This Isn't It

> *"Once you get to the top of the mountain, you still have to get down."*

This important and eye-opening chapter may, in a sense, be especially relevant to you. As I've said, I spent ten years on the road as a comedy stage hypnotist doing crazy things to those under my spell. The story of how this came to be was a huge lesson for me, as I was at a major crossroad in my life.

I had been selling insurance in Nebraska. But I got to a point where I knew this was not *me*. Selling long-term insurance to farmers wasn't allowing me to live in my gift zone.

I'd ask myself, every day, what I should do. What opportunity would show up? I engaged the L.O.M. (Law of Manifestation, remember?) and began to hone in on my talents, skills, energy and passion.

After a few months, Rhonda and I decided to go to Las Vegas for a night. We searched for a show to attend after dinner. Because we visited Las Vegas frequently, we'd seen most of the shows. But a show called *Hypnosis Unleashed* caught my eye.

As I explained to Rhonda, a hypnotist's show is built around putting audience volunteers in a state where they'll do crazy things. Rhonda wasn't too thrilled to see this, but something within me said I should attend.

Standing in line for tickets, someone tapped me on the shoulder and asked, "Are you here for my show?" My show? This man was Michael Johns. And yes, it was his show.

We had a lot in common. We both had a military background, both had played in a band, and both were outgoing. Still in line, I told him that I would love to learn how to do what he did. I was fascinated—I still am—with how the mind works and frequently read up on the power of the mind.

I think Michael was surprised, but he offered to meet after the show to talk further. I agreed, still in shock. Inside, he sat us in a special section and suggested I take notes. Always the student, this was perfect for me.

After the show, we met at a little café in the casino. Conversation with him was so easy it felt like we were old friends. Here was a guy that worked in Vegas doing comedy very successfully and I was telling him about my background and my love of performing in front of an audience, motivating, selling and getting people to take action to improve their lives.

After a few hours, ready to say our goodbyes, he asked if I was serious about learning the craft. I was. We decided to meet for lunch the very next day.

So, what had just happened? I had just met this guy who would take me somewhere I'd never been before. I knew the Law of Manifestation had worked quickly to pave out a new path for me. I was so excited I barely slept.

We met at a burger joint. Here, Michael became my teacher. He said, "Many come to me and pay good money for me to instruct them. But most waste my time. So, here's my proposition: I'm going to mentor you if you do some specific things. If and when you do them, we'll reconnect to discuss the next step. Tony, I have a good feeling about you. I have a feeling you won't waste my time. And, I'm going to do this for free."

I told him how grateful and honored I was. And I would not, for sure, waste his time. I would do the work and reconnect as soon as my work was completed.

My heart raced. But I was at peace with the decision even if I didn't quite know what I was letting myself in for. I trusted my gut.

He wanted me to read *Hypnotherapy* by Dave Elman (the bible for those who want to understand hypnosis), among other research projects.

Rhonda told me I'd be perfect for this; entertaining would be right up my alley. Excited about my new direction, I dove into the research.

Later, Michael quizzed me at length, then announced he was proud that I'd followed his directions. He also said that when his show came near Nebraska, I could come see him perform again, this time with an eye to becoming a performer myself.

A few months passed before I heard from him again. I was still selling insurance, doing okay but still unhappy doing so. He'd be in Iowa for three shows. There, I could begin training. I cleared my schedule and off I went.

He allowed me to videotape his shows and take all the notes I needed. I was back in student mode, working with a master.

I documented everything: the time he woke up, his pre-show routine, his checklist, the music selections, the seating arrangement, everything from when the doors opened to when they closed. No detail was left out. I knew from experience that Michael controlled the whole show experience and I wanted to figure it out in order to learn from it.

I was in awe of both him and the show. How could he possibly take an audience of skeptics and create a 90-minute show that removed all doubt? It's magical, believe me.

I spent three days, asking innumerable questions, dissecting everything to make sure I understood it all. After I thanked him for the amazing opportunity, we parted, promising to keep in touch. I had no idea how this would unfold, but it seemed that Rhonda had become the messenger, and manager, for what would come next.

On my way home, she asked how it went. I told her that Michael was amazing to work with. She wanted to know if I actually considered doing this for real. I did. But something was up with her. Sure enough, there was. That Sunday at the Joyo Theatre in Lincoln, she'd booked me as the headliner for their comedy show.

In four days! I'd never hypnotized anyone yet. I was just barely an apprentice, still learning, understanding, reviewing, questioning, studying—this Sunday? Like in four days? I couldn't believe she'd done that!

But, when the Law of Manifestation kicks in, it delivers at warp speed. I had four days to develop a show, get my skills actually working properly, and deliver something worth seeing.

I parked myself in front of my TV and ran the videos from Michael's shows. I decided to copy one verbatim. My pre-talk, my intro, everything, would be a carbon copy.

Now, who was I going to be? What would the audience know me as? After much thought I decided on the name Mojo. After all, I needed my mojo working overtime to get through this. So, I became Mojo Master.

I practiced the intro—to relax potential volunteers—on my dog, my daughter, Rhonda, even on me via a mirror. I took over the basement and practiced everything until it became smooth as silk.

Believe it or not, the hardest part was deciding what to wear. What was my image? What persona did I want to create? What was my vibe? I decided I wanted to be a rock star, complete with an upbeat soundtrack and loads of energy. The audience would feel my mojo, feel my energy and the energy of the show from the time they entered until long after they exited. I wanted to make such an impact that they'd talk about my show for months.

The night of the show, I went through all my pre-show checks as the audience filed in. Rhonda had me billed as a famous hypnotist from Las Vegas who lived locally. Luckily, most were excited to see something different. And I was ready to deliver.

I asked a local comedian to do some standup for the first ten minutes. When I hit the stage I felt at peace—I was ready and the audience was primed for a good show.

I explained how the show would proceed and asked for some volunteers. Sixteen came up. I kept twelve. And, lo and behold, I successfully hypnotized them all. Crazy what you can accomplish in four days!

I got a standing ovation.

I thanked everyone, overwhelmed at the response, and went backstage to be alone. I knelt, tears in my eyes, so emotional, looked up and said to myself that I should be doing this for the rest of my life. I was endlessly grateful that the universe had delivered Michael to me and I could entertain an audience with my skills. I was truly fulfilled. And I would be a world-class hypnotist.

I toured for ten years, with up to 250 shows a year, from New York to Vegas and back. I became one of the top requested performers, had thousands of fans, and spent quite a bit of time on the road away from my family. When I reached the financial ceiling, the show, and me, lost its sizzle. The only way to do more, achieve more, would be to spend even more time away from home. That was not an option.

I asked myself if entertaining was my purpose. Personally, I enjoyed performing. I loved the travel, the people, and creating laughter. But something was missing. There must be more just over the horizon.

During this exciting decade, I learned that my life was solid confirmation that the Law of Manifestation, choosing, following my gut, and finding a mentor were indeed very powerful forces that, when acknowledged and implemented, truly worked in unison to enrich my life.

My lesson to you: Trust. Don't be afraid of the speed in which the universe offers opportunity after opportunity. Trust.

16

Let the Healing Begin

"There is a doctor in your house."

What if I told you you could heal yourself—both mind *and* body?

What I'm about to share is, on the surface, somewhat nonsensical. But you'll soon see that humans can heal all aspects of their lives. Get ready, because your special powers are about to be revealed.

The best doctor in existence is you.

The energy contained in our bodies could light up the city of Las Vegas. We're complex creatures with enormous potential. If we used more than just five to ten percent of our brainpower, the idea of superhero-type actions might be easily accepted. It's not.

Our current reality deals only in what we know and in what we can see. The idea of healing oneself is not a topic we spend much time on. It's so much easier just to get advice from a doctor, friend, or from something we read. We just bandage uncomfortable situations with medication. Once we understand our superpowers, that there's no limit to what we can do, then the idea of healing oneself should make sense. Here is my story.

I've been very active my whole life. Five hours of sleep is enough. I wake up and start moving almost immediately. And for the last ten years, I've begun my mornings with a regiment.

I've read books on meditation, yoga, and other modalities to tap into the spiritual connection with self and the universe.

My daily routine is geared to specifically create an energy of positivity, health, vitality and productivity. In a sense, I begin each day my way. I don't get whisked away in a vortex of chaos.

I start when I'm ready. Sometimes this takes five minutes, sometimes thirty. I won't jump the gun. It's not a race.

And to make this easy for you, I'm going to share what exactly I do before I go to bed and what I do when I rise.

Remember, I've done all the work for you. You, as student, only need to put it into practice. Interestingly enough, I felt myself heal over a period of years. My vitality is better today—I'm over 50—than it was 30 years ago.

This healing routine must be followed consistently—not just when it's convenient or you feel like it. I'll share the issues that crop up, then show you how, through certain habitual actions, I was able to change the outcome from what might have happened to what I manifested to happen.

As we get older, our bodies require more time and effort to recover. But sometimes, my mind doesn't communicate with my body properly and I go full out. Usually, I end up hurting myself.

Playing basketball with college kids at 50 is not the best idea, but I have a competitive side to assuage. I played basketball for the Air Force and I still enjoy running the floor to this day.

I have two big dogs that I train and exercise every day. Louis, my huge 80-pound Staffordshire Bull Terrier, sometimes gets distracted when we walk and I find myself going one way while he goes another. One day we were hiking together, descending a hill. Something got his attention and he went off. I lost my balance and slipped on a rock. My knee twisted. When I put pressure on it, I got a sharp pain.

At home, I covered my knee with ice and took it easy. After, I still felt the pain—like a needle between my knee bones. The ice helped some. Over time, I just learned to live with it. Somedays it felt fine, other days the weather seemed to affect it. Certainly, there was an issue. So I began each morning with a more focused intent to heal myself. Over time, it's evolved into the routine described below.

These days, before I jump out of bed, I just lie there, awake. I know there's lots to do: check my social media feeds, workout, make coffee, whatever. But I can do those later.

This is what I do:

1. Eyes closed, I acknowledge ten things I'm grateful for at this moment: people, my health, the air, the bed I'm in, my finances, whatever comes up. I

welcome those and I'm grateful. Gratitude affects your attitude, remember. The more grateful I am for the *things* in my life, the better my attitude.

2. I stay very quiet, meditate and ask the divine to scan my body and, with the love I feel for myself and others, heal my ailments. Anything that my body, mind and spirit needs, I ask that love to heal me. (In the case of my knee, I would focus on a white light sending energy in the form of love to nourish it, to give it more oxygen, more blood, more love to heal it.)

3. I tell myself that today, people, events and ideas that I am ready for at this moment, are going to show up if needed. I'm telling the universe that whatever I need to experience today will be a gift that I get to open tomorrow.

4. Finally, I see the beauty in everything and everyone. Look around your environment; beauty is everywhere. If you don't believe me, go look in the mirror, or look outside, or at the pictures on your wall. Beauty is everywhere, I can assure you. I'll detail more of this in the workbook section.

To show you how effective this is, after I injured my knee I remained active, healing my knee every night and every morning, sending it love while visualizing a white beam of light.

My wife, the caring soul that she is, said I needed to get it looked at by a professional to make sure nothing major was wrong. I had an MRI done and was sent to a therapist for diagnosis. I had a torn meniscus. Surgery was recommended because the tear was in a bad location and, in order for it to heal, the area needed a great deal of blood and oxygen. At 50, recovery would be slow. I would be in constant pain and it would likely get worse if I stayed active.

So, how was I to get more blood and oxygen to the injury? I began to do some research. I read how some were able to focus their energy and do miraculous things. I decided to try that.

What follows is what I did for a minimum of twice daily, each session lasting ten minutes. *Minimum*, remember?

I'd lay down, comfortable, and place one hand on my heart and the other on my knee. I thought how much I loved myself and how truly grateful I was for all my experiences. I would tell my heart to send love to my knee. I would tell it to send as much blood and oxygen as the injury needed. I would imagine and visualize blood flowing from my heart, down my arm to the knee. At the same time, I felt real love for what was happening.

Many times, I became so happy knowing what I was doing for myself that I would begin to cry. So much love was flowing through me. I felt honored that I had this time alone so I could focus on no one else but me. I visualized blood moving over the torn area and feeding it the nutrients it needed.

I continued this, every single day, for about 40 days. The pain slowly left. Walking became normal. There was no swelling. And I'd lost the excuse not to exercise.

I had done what my therapist said could not be done. I can say now that I'm fully healed, this after 90 days of loving myself. And the only way I could have discovered this technique was by being awake, or aware, of the possibilities.

What are you dealing with that continues to plague you? Is it your back? Headaches? Knee pain? Every day, begin with this regimen. Pretend they are doctor's orders. Every morning and night, bring your loving energy to the area you want to heal. Be consistent and let the healing take place. This, combined with wholesome nutrition, great attitude and happy environment, will create miracles.

17

Peru

"In order to see things in a different light, a different light must shine."

I know you're ready for what comes next. We've gone over a wide variety of simple topics, every chapter giving you food for thought with techniques and strategies to apply to your own life.

This book is a blueprint, a journal, and reveals the precise formula for you to manifest abundance, give you inspiration, and shows you the next steps for your journey to discovery of self-purpose.

The exercises, if you've done them, have created a force field around you. When put into daily practice, they'll make you oblivious to what's happening around you. Inside you is the world that really matters. The better the harvest of your personal garden, the more beautiful the outside world becomes. You'll be laser-focused and become a better version of yourself.

One of my favorite quotes comes from the movie *The Shawshank Redemption*. The character Andy Dufresne says, "Get busy living, or get busy dying." You're now living and alive with life. You're not settling, not giving in, not buying into the gossip negativity that may have damaged you before. You've seen the light, and maybe stepped out into it. This light is now waiting for you. Now is the time to spread your wings and ascend as high as you can.

The next few chapters depict the time I was in my incubation period. It was a year in my life that everything I had learned, everything I had experienced, hit me on the head and allowed me to go on.

What you're about to read are accounts of two different journeys to the most powerful place on the planet, as far as energy is concerned. This place is Peru.

Sit back and enjoy the true events that precipitated my birth as a Kondor.

The Beginning of Something Big

In 2015, having just turned 50, I hit the peak of my current business venture. It had made me millions. I lived in a beautiful home on the cliffs of San Diego, had two acres to play in, enjoyed a quiet life behind security gates, drove supercars, and loved the fabulous weather. It was a life people dream about. And I was living it.

We had a great friend living with us, nourishing us with vegan meals and great conversation. We were on autopilot, a place everyone is at some point in their lives. Yet, something was missing.

Every day, I continued to work on myself, then started to ask myself what the second half of my life should look like. What was the true purpose for me being here? I'd weathered quite a few storms yet managed to keep everything together. But my purpose? What about my legacy? What are my kids, and their kids, going to say about me? Being 50 does something to a man.

I meditated, sometimes three times a day, asking for guidance. I wanted to contribute to the world. Throughout my life, I've always felt that I was being tested for something. Something big.

In December, we decided to throw a party. We'd just had a fantastic year and we wanted to celebrate it.

Some clients had expressed a desire for an East Asian Bali theme. We planned to gather lots of sheer fabric, play great music and have special lighting. The food would be beyond exquisite. We also wanted to serve our guests in a way that would enliven all their senses. In all, we wanted to create an event that would be talked about for a good long time.

Many of the 35 guests were strangers to mc, but I trusted they were the right people. They turned out to be an eclectic group of professionals, artists and spiritual beings. They were simply beautiful. Everything was perfect.

As the guests arrived, Rhonda and I mingled. What got my attention were two words from random conversations. Every time I heard them, they seemed separated from the rest of the conversation—like they were five octaves higher. The words were Peru and Ayahuasca.

Why was I noticing these two words? What did they mean? Was this a message meant for me? Instantly, I was fully awake, my superpowers alerted. I decided I should ask questions.

The more I investigated, the more those words became significant, and the more I became excited. From complete strangers, I found out that Peru is the world's number one energy center. There's energy from the earth, healing energy, and powerful forces and frequencies that affect both the locals and visitors.

In Peru, the Amazon River and the jungle combine to form a unique ecosystem. The sheer number of different species of animals, insects and plants is unlike any other place. It's magical.

Many of the plants are called *power plants*. They have the ability to heal sickness, both mental and physical. The Mother of all these power plants is Mother Ayahuasca. Under the right conditions and preparation, this plant has a most profound effect—hence the name "Mother."

Ayahuasca will show you the true essence of your soul in a way that the regular mind cannot explain. She'll allow you to confront the events, people and situations you need in order to advance to what you're seeking.

Let me say right away, I don't do drugs and I only drink wine occasionally. The idea of ingesting Ayahuasca and facing potentially psychedelic demons I wasn't aware of scared me.

I asked my heart, “What do you want me to do?” My heart, without missing a beat, said, “Go to Peru and allow Mother Ayahuasca to assist you on your path to purpose.” I didn’t know anything about Ayahuasca, so I had to do some research online.

After viewing a few videos, I wondered what the heck I was getting myself into. Many showed users purging (a nice word for puking), freaking out and wrestling with their demons. Could this be what it’s really like? Maybe it was just the experience of a few. I had to investigate further.

I contacted the guests from my party. All of them said it was a beautiful experience, but, they cautioned, you’ll have to deal with things that are uncomfortable. They advised me to make peace with those and learn from them.

The Ayahuasca ceremony lasts between five and seven hours. Seven whole hours of demon hunting? I had to focus on the beautiful experiences my guests all had. My heart said I needed to go. So I made plans. But I didn’t share those awful videos with my wife and son until I left. My guess, they would have attempted to talk me out of it. I began my research on where I should go.

There were so many retreats that had started in the jungle and surrounding areas that it was hard to choose. I meditated to find the one retreat center that would be the best for me. I found it. Because of the respect I have for this center, I will not reveal its name here. But I will acknowledge them for the great work and environment they’ve created in the Amazon for those that attend.

I felt safe, welcomed, and respected for what I was about to do. When I contacted them, they said there were no openings until June. This was December and I’m an impatient man. I asked them to keep me in mind if an earlier opening came up. Anytime.

I finished out the year, doing research all the while. I began to feel quite comfortable about my decision, although I've never been separated from my family, far away in a place I'd never been. I waited, impatiently, and researched.

On January 8, I received an email from the center saying there was a February opening. They wanted a quick response because they had a long waiting list. My schedule happened to be clear, so I booked.

Six days in the Amazon jungle with nothing but five pairs of underwear, four shirts, sandals, toiletries, a journal and a head lamp—this was going to be interesting. I prepared myself for three Ayahuasca ceremonies.

My diet had to be clean—no meats, greasy foods, salt etc. for five days before arrival. My OCD kicked in. I wanted to make sure I did everything the best I could. I wanted to truly honor Mother Ayahuasca and the whole experience so that I could get the most out of it. I began journaling and soon my journal was starting to come to life. I'll explain.

They say that once you've committed to experiencing Ayahuasca, Mother starts to communicate with you through dreams, thoughts, and even visions while awake. I can tell you that this is true. I was drawing pictures in my journal that made no sense at the time. My night dreams were unlike any I've ever had. They were brighter, more futuristic, like I'd been transported to another dimension.

I began to get very emotional. I would see a sunset and tears would come to my eyes. Certain TV commercials would make me cry. I wondered what was happening to me.

All I can say is that it was beautiful. I was being prepared for something wonderful. My diet was now clean, my mind ready and the excitement of going to a place I'd never been was almost more invigorating than I could stand.

Saying goodbye to Rhonda was very difficult. Once I'd left the U.S., I would be off the grid; jungle cell phone coverage is very limited.

I arrived at my destination after an all-night flight. The airport was chaotic, everyone yelling for rides, tours, drinks and jewelry. It was very fast moving. A driver was sent to pick me up; he took me deep into the jungle.

A Magical Place

The jungle was awesome. The sounds, the colors, everything so vibrant it was hard to take in.

After introductions with the director and assistant, I was taken to my home for the week—a simple hut with roof, floor, screens to keep bugs out, a bed and table, and a simple hole for a latrine. That's it.

The basic conditions were precisely what I'd hoped for. They were the exact opposite of my normal situation. I settled in and got ready for the evening ceremony.

My group, all new attendees, joined those already there. Two members had been there over a month, working with the Ayahuasca plant that whole time. Obviously their problems were very deep-rooted.

After a briefing on what was to take place, I gathered my journal, bottled water and good attitude and walked to the Maloka center.

The ritual began with a cleansing of our space using Palo Santo wood and Florida water. The burning wood gave off a most wonderful scent. Before drinking our shot of Ayahuasca, we had to state our intentions. Mine was to deal with anything from my past that I was holding onto, unaware of or needing to face. Ayahuasca is thick like molasses and rather grainy with a taste that's hard to describe.

We were instructed to sit on our mats and stay silent until our Shaman finished singing. As soon as I drank, the fire was put out. You couldn't see your hand in front of your face. Then a crash of thunder, the loudest I've ever heard—and I've lived in Nebraska! Then the rain began, hard.

Obviously Mother Nature and Mother Ayahuasca had something to say. I felt like I was in a movie—a very scary one—as the rain, thunder and wind continued to roar. I closed my eyes and something strange happened.

I was in another place, a dimension that was simply peace, like one I'd never felt. I could hear my heartbeat and saw stars, some like neon—pinks, blues, yellows and greens. To my left, a light approached, attached to a huge hand. Then I saw the most beautiful thing I have ever seen—a woman with beautiful, blue eyes. Her face and body were translucent, like that of a jelly fish at night with a light shining on it. At the end of her fingertips were these little different colored neon lights.

Her whole face glowed, her body floating. Her hands touched my body very gently, but just on certain places: my knee, ankle, thigh, heart, throat, eyes and forehead. She touched so gently, so slowly, as if to scan and heal any issues I might have had. She floated effortlessly over me, blinking long slow blinks, each touch very real—I could feel each place begin to vibrate, along with hearing a deep humming.

I did not want it to end. I felt the love and care she gave me. I was so very grateful. I've never felt so connected with myself and to a love like this. I knew what heaven was and I was elated. Moments after her last touch, she stared at me, blinked a couple times as if to say all is well. I love you.

She vanished into the distance and darkness enveloped me once again. I lost sense of where I was. But then it began—I was moments from facing the demons in my past. I was in a hallway, both sides covered with black, moving heads, mouths opening and closing and spitting at me. These were the faceless people in my life that at some point had belittled me, doubted me, hated me, were jealous of me and hurt me. I had come face to face with those that attempted to damage me.

Then the whole place changed colors, filled with different textures and shapes. Snakes appeared and wrapped themselves around my feet. The ground became bumpy, slick looking, and covered in dirty moss. Trees lashed out at me.

I was in another dimension. My brain dealt with all the ugliness, anger and disappointment that I still carried. As I attempted to make sense of it, the need to purge arose. Strange, despite all the unreality, I still knew where my bucket was. Stranger, I didn't mind purging. After all, I was being guided to face a different and rapidly changing environment. Things would just pop in and out. Colors too, then blackness.

Mother had taken me deep into my own brain. And it housed people and events that I never knew existed. I was facing them head on and purging them out of existence. It was so beautiful.

Remember my intention of getting rid of what I was holding on to? I was in for a big surprise. I'd just finished purging when a twenty-foot figure in a black cape loomed up before me. George. He'd come to confront me one more time.

He swung out at me, spitting, mouth open like a great white shark, ready to eat me whole. I stood and readied for battle. I told him he had no more power over me. Nothing about him—his memories, his actions, his voice—affected me. I began to spit back and a small light flashed on, a voice asking, "Tony, are you all right?" I said I was, that I was dealing with something big. The voice said it understood, but I should stop spitting and sit back down.

The staff always seem to be there when you needed them. I thanked them and sat. Then I purged George into the darkness. Just when I thought I was done, the lesson of all lessons appeared.

Rhonda had two children from a prior marriage. Along with their biological father, I helped raise them. The oldest, Kaleb, was six when Rhonda and I got together; the youngest Kamryn, was four. As the kids moved into high school, I couldn't relate to some of the many parenting situations Rhonda and her ex had to deal with. You see, I was oblivious to how other children were raised. For that reason, I felt myself pulling away from Rhonda and her children.

Because we were financially stable and loved one another, Rhonda believed the children shouldn't have to worry about anything. But to me, if a child doesn't face adversity and responsibility, he or she will never be able to cope with difficult situations.

I saw our family unravel in front of me, but I couldn't step in and be that bad guy that seemed to always teach them to accept the responsibilities and deal with the challenges. They were growing to despise me—the enforcer. That set up what happened next.

Kaleb, at 18, got his 17-year-old girlfriend pregnant. This disrupted our household. I really had a hard time with this. Rhonda wanted the baby brought up in a safe home. And so, our monthly budget now included the girlfriend and her baby.

I'd seen this kind of thing coming for years. Now I was living it. My relationship with Rhonda changed. I felt numb, then angry, disappointed and shamed. Every time someone asked how the family was doing, I relived this.

Back in the jungle, having purged once more, I saw Kaleb's face. I got angry again, disappointed, frustrated and lost. Crying, I said, "Why. Why Kaleb, why?" Kaleb just stared at me. This went on for a time. In that dimension, time had no meaning—it didn't exist. I could have been at it for five minutes or five hours. My stomach was in knots, my tears flowed freely like a child's, then I was gagging, unable to purge. I wanted it to stop. I felt myself collapse, drift down, mentally and physically drained. "Why? Why Kaleb?"

Just when I was at my lowest, I heard the sweetest child's voice in the distance. "Let it go. Let it go." Music from the movie *Frozen*. I raised my head and Sofia, my granddaughter, faced me, singing, then said, "Hi Pappi." At two, that's what she called me. I was not Grandpa. So Pappi was it.

"Pappi, you have to let it go. Let it go, Pappi!" She began singing to me again. "Let it go. Let it go." I knew I had to listen to this angel and let it go. I looked at Kaleb again, still crying, and said, "Kaleb, I see so much beauty and potential in you. I love you and I truly forgive you. I'm asking for you to forgive me too. I'm so sorry, son. I'm going to let it go.

I love you and I'm so very, very sorry." At that moment, I purged for the last time. As I lay weeping, my son Tony (12 years old) appeared and sat next to me, rubbed my head and said, "Dad, you're so strong a dad. You're like a superhero. I am so proud of you. Wow, Dad. I'm so proud."

I remember being at peace with what had transpired. I had no more strength, no mental energy. I simply lay there and cried tears of happiness until I fell asleep. It was the most magical, beautiful experience of my life.

The next morning, I felt so much lighter. I was still emotional from what I'd just gone through and began to journal about the session. I just couldn't believe that a natural plant could show you this. The emotional healing someone can experience if they're willing to experience Ayahuasca is better than 15 years of psychiatric counseling, and a whole lot cheaper. I was a new man, with a new outlook and appreciation for Mother, the universe and all of us as humans.

I was proud of myself for going through this. I needed it. It was important that I grow. But this was only the first of three ceremonies. I couldn't wait for the next one. But for now, I had a day to recover, to be at one with nature, to journal, and to go deeper into myself than ever before.

My light was brighter than ever; I liked what I had found. And Wednesday would be an opportunity to find out what my purpose was.

Becoming a Lion

Wednesday, before I drank, I asked for guidance and took a position next to the director of the retreat—an honor.

On my mat, I offered gratitude to Mother Ayahuasca for what she'd done for me and what she was about to show me. My heart was full.

As the plant's magic began, a new scene presented itself. I saw a man, very shiny, metallic looking, with glowing eyes and a sculpted face. When he placed his hands on me, I relaxed and felt as I had the last time. The vibrations were just as strong on my knee, chest, heart, throat, eyes and head. I truly enjoyed this. There was so much love, I knew I was okay. Then, just as I got comfortable, it went dark.

A loud female voice said, "Tony, are you ready?" I said, "Yes." "Tony, are you really ready? And do you trust me?" I said yes to both, recalling that the previous time she'd taught me the true meaning of trust.

She gave me very specific directions. "Exhale all your air. All of it, until there's nothing left." I did this and she said, "More, Tony. Expel more air; let it all out. You still have more air." I squeezed out a little more. "More, Tony. You still have more inside you." I tried to push out more. Finally, she said, "Good, now hold your breath." I was like, what breath? I had none. "Relax, Tony. Just relax. Do you trust me? Just relax. Keep holding it." I held my breath for what seemed like an hour. My stomach hurt, my face hurt, everything hurt, but I kept holding my breath. "Breathe, Tony." I did. I gasped to get air into my lungs as fast as possible. Once I recovered, she said, "Again Tony, push out your air, as much as you can." Again I exhaled, squeezing every little bit. I now knew what she expected. We did this exercise no less than ten times, testing me, teaching me something.

I was then instructed to inhale, to fill my diaphragm with air and hold it. What a switch. "Inhale more, Tony." More? "Now hold your breath. Keep holding." I trusted and held, and held, and held for what seemed like 30 minutes. In this dimension, it's crazy what you can do. "Let it out." I did, trying to get my lungs back to normal.

We repeated this ten times or more. I was physically exhausted. Then she said, "You're ready!" I had learned to trust in a very powerful way. I could have taken a breath very easily, but I realized if I was to truly deserve what I was about to be taught, I had to build a trust and prove to myself that I deserved this. Mother was now ready to teach me what I wanted to see.

She had me get up on all fours, like a dog. "Tony, make your shoulders strong. Make them strong as you press into the ground." I did and she kept saying to make them stronger. "Stronger, Tony. You've always said you have weak shoulders. Make them strong. Flex those shoulders as you press into the ground." This went on for several minutes, me on all fours with strong, flexed shoulders. She asked that I move my head to the left and right as if I was gazing over a cliff to a valley below. We continued this for quite some time, until she was satisfied with her little puppet. I was directed to lay down.

It's here she began to speak to me in a very soft voice. I could feel the sweat dripping from my face—I had expended quite a bit of energy to maintain my position. Mother said, "Tony, for your whole life, you've been cute—like a Tiger. Your mom called you "Tony the Tiger" while you ate "Tony the Tiger" cereal. You've been a baby cub, then a tiger. Tonight, you're a Lion—the most respected and loyal creature on land. You're a mighty lion. You'll now roam the earth, strong, proud, and respected immediately by all who meet you. You're a lion, Tony. A lion."

In tears, my whole life flashed in front of me—all the things I'd conquered, how strong I was, everything. I was indeed a lion. It was official. And I was ready to show the world my strength. My first role was to help the others that were here in the Maloka.

The person next to me was a kid in his twenties, named Jonas. Even though I couldn't see him well in the darkness, I knew he was having a problem purging. He was very uncomfortable—hyperventilating.

I sat up, strong as a lion, and whispered in a firm voice, "Jonas, listen to me. I need you to follow my breathing." He was so out of it, he didn't respond. I kept at him until he said, "Okay." I began to show him how to breathe—slowly at first, very controlled and aware, exhaling through the mouth, inhaling through the nose. He followed my example. But when I asked him to sit up, he just stayed hunched over like all his fight had gone.

The director intervened, hushing us. Without looking up, I raised my left paw and made him leave us. He simply walked away. I was a lion and I was teaching. I couldn't be bothered with him right now. I was doing what Mother wanted.

I asked Jonas to sit up, to be strong and take back his power. I told him I saw a strong man, not a weak child. He was a beautiful creature capable of so much love. I believed in him. He sat up and after about five minutes began to purge.

I left him and spent the rest of the night in the position of a lion observing and assisting others without words, simply listening and directing positive energy in their direction. I could feel what they were going through. Simply by focusing on them, I could help them have a breakthrough. In the darkness, I focused my love for them with great intent. I listened as their troubles faded away. One by one, they all purged. I was grateful to be the king. I felt their beauty in what they were doing and I loved each of them for the journey they were on.

Hours went by. I was emotionally drained from harnessing all that emotion and extending my focus. I lay down, tears in my eyes. I knew that I was here to offer hope to the world, to heal with my love and to show others how to do the same. I was a proud lion.

As I lay there, Mother said, "Do you want to see something cool?" Of course, I would. She asked that I look up into the darkness. The roof of the Maloka was filled with beautiful geometric shapes. All of a sudden, the shape of a man's head appeared. I asked what it was. "Tony can you keep a secret?" "Of course I can, Mother."

"Tony, what you're looking at is me. I'm not Mother; I'm your father. I'm the father you never had, the father whose voice you heard guiding you all those years. I'm your father that will now be with you every step of the way, to help you guide others. I'm so very proud of all the work you've done in your life. You've made all of us very proud. Sleep, my son. Tomorrow you'll tell the director that you've received what you were seeking. You're a healer of millions and you'll not be doing another Ayahuasca ceremony. However, I need you to be part of the ceremony to practice what you've learned and focus on assisting others, as there is much work to do. The director will not agree with this, but you have to be a lion and tell him my word has to be honored."

I was to assist in the ceremony and never again have to experience Ayahuasca. I was going to be a healer of millions. Wow, what a wakeup call. I had better get to work.

I was very excited to take on my new responsibilities. My whole life, I have healed people, in a sense. Through my music, my ten years as a hypnotist, my connection with people, my experiences and my ability to listen and offer my counsel. I was now to do this on a much bigger platform. And I was readier than ever.

Sharing the Magic

Friday's ceremony began the same way as the previous two. Once again, I was in the honored position, sitting next to the director. As this was the last night for many, whatever work they had left had to be completed.

I'd said to Jonas earlier that he was hiding behind his long hair. Seeing his huge smile would be wonderful. In response, he shaved his head. The women likened him to Brad Pitt. Apparently, this was the first time he'd smiled since arriving. In his hut, we spent an hour talking about his life. I mostly listened.

He admitted he was a troubled kid. His mother worried about everything and kept him isolated. He couldn't remember the last time he'd laughed. I asked him to concentrate on laughing during the ceremony. He agreed to try.

Once my eyes adjusted to the darkness, I could see the outlines of the other seven. Some were lying down, others sat. For the first time, I could make this all out. Maybe I could see in the dark?

When I looked about the room, I made out red and yellow shapes, like cells from high school biology. This is where their pain came from. Some had cells on their stomachs, some on their backs, some on their heads—all areas that needed attention.

Jonas had cells up and down his throat and stomach. I sent him love and energy. I focused my breathing and attention on his pain. I visualized a white light touching his stomach and breaking up those clogs of color. I sent more love, more energy, more attention and began to work on his throat. Love, breath, energy and light.

Father guided me. Everything I did was orchestrated. I felt the power of the lion.

The red and yellow colors became less intense, yet I continued to work with focus and love. Focused love. The red faded and changed to a greenish color. Then to a real green. I began to cry.

Jonas started to breathe slowly, easily, and began to cry. No words were exchanged; it was just me sending him focused love. The colors were now all green, even on his throat.

This process took a few hours. Since I was completely present, completely focused, all that time, it felt even longer. Once all the colors had changed to green, I lay down and rested. I heard the door of the Maloka close and a minute later heard laughter coming from outside.

The laughter gradually got louder and louder, then hysterical. All of us in the Maloka started to laugh. For that one moment,

Father let us all celebrate. No matter what we were dealing with, we got to share some laughter. Jonas had discovered his laughter. He laughed for 30 minutes straight, so long the director had to check to make sure he was okay. He was more than okay.

I walked back to my hut as the sun rose. I wanted to document everything. I could see the power of love. I could see and feel it. I understood what I had discovered a long while ago—we all have the ability to heal ourselves and others. Now confirmed, it was time to develop this new superpower and put it to use. I will teach you this power at the end of this book. For now, just know there is power in love.

When I share this moment of my life with others, I'm instantly transported to that time and place. Words will never be able to articulate how wonderful an experience this was. All I can say is that there are different dimensions which house different realities. Sometimes we have to do something like fly to Peru and live with ourselves in the jungle in order to realize how much we don't know and how much more we need to know.

18

Get Back in the Game

"Who you were is not who you are."

The journey home was emotional. I was only gone a week but it felt like an eternity. My discovery of self, assisted by Father, was like a four-year Master's degree crammed into a few days. I was so grateful to have gone through the experience. Now, I had to implement.

My big lesson from this: it's one thing to know how to change; it's another to actually go and do it. I had to get home and get moving. Remember, the universe loves speed and activity.

The plan was to create a space in my house where I could develop and hone my skills on my close friends.

After the room was set up, the name of my little center decided upon, I began to share my discoveries with those friends. Rhonda loved the work I did with her. I truly believed she made up ailments, issues, aches, pains etc., just so I could give her some attention. Heck, I would have done the same thing. I had no issue with it. I enjoyed making her feel focused love. Isn't that what we all want?

After a month or so, our other business demands started to pull me away from my new practice. I was torn. Do I support the business that supplied our income or do I pursue my new venture? This battle continued for another month and finally, out of support for our team and obligations, I made the decision to go back to our business and focus my energy there. I left what I had just learned on the shelf.

My heart was in alignment with this. I knew when the time was right, I could jump back into my newly discovered work. Sometimes you have to make sacrifices to the whole in order to become whole again. In life, this often happens. I understood that this decision was forced upon me for a reason. Very soon, I'd know why I'd been pulled away from what I just learned. I meditated about it and my heart was fine. I had to trust that I was being guided and I had to let it go.

Months passed and our business started to get back on track. In quiet moments, I heard the call to do more work on that self.

My biggest discoveries, who I was and what my purpose was, were being cultivated. I would soon be asked to take a journey that would answer all my questions and lay out the roadmap for how I was to spend the rest of my life. I was going to unveil my opus, my masterpiece, to share with the world and impact many lives—millions of them.

What I'm about to share with you is 50, or rather, 100 or more years in the making. It's my final 20 days of incubation.

It's the Birth of a Kondor.

19

The Sequel, Peru Again

"Discover your soul's desire and live a life of abundance."

Answers come to you when you're awake, not asleep. My heart was once again ready to discover more, experience more, love more.

Peru had such an impact on me the first time that I knew it would offer even more the second time around. As I continued to practice my improved superpowers, I, more than ever, stayed connected to myself and observed the signs around me. Many were leading me to the energy that was only available in the Andes. I couldn't deny that my next step was to plan, not so much a journey, but a pilgrimage to the sacred power places of Peru.

Power places are best described as geographical areas where sacred events have taken place. In these places, the divine is acknowledged through prayer, offerings and love. I would come to know that the Andeans believed that Mother Earth (Pachamama) was born there. Also, the true masters and teachers of our history did their work in Peru. I would discover what turned out to be the most defining moment of my life. Hang on, leave your passport at home, we're going to the destination where life began.

Imagine a conversation with your significant other where you say that you're going off to Peru, flying with a one-way ticket because you have no firm return date, need camping gear, know no one there, will leave within three weeks and it's something that you absolutely must do. I had this conversation just before the Christmas holidays. By January 5, I would be on a plane.

In a quiet moment, Machu Picchu, the Crystal City, came to me. The Andeans believe it's one of the most sacred centers in their culture. Machu Picchu, if inhabited today, would be the "perfect" city. The loyalty, hard work and love that went into the creation of that city is how we should base communities of today. It was, and still is, perfect.

The only things on my agenda were a four-day Inca Trail hike to visit the sacred city and time to spend there. I added another day's hike to Huayna Picchu to make an offering to the world. I was advised to be on Huayna Picchu's summit at 10 a.m. EST on January 14. I was ecstatic, knowing that I was being led. I was a kid on a solo roller coaster ride. Waiting to leave, the days dragged very slowly.

On this trip, instead of going into the Amazon jungle, I would travel to the city of Cusco. Cusco radiates such energy that people come from all over the world to feel connected. In my research, I came across a video of a gentleman with long grey and black hair being interviewed in a canoe on a lake.

He seemed very knowledgeable about the Andean culture, energy, and power places. I could feel his passion and love for the Andes. He was someone I wanted to meet—I just didn't know how yet. I didn't even know if he lived anywhere close. So I tapped into my special powers, utilized the Law of Manifestation and sent my energy to the universe and just trusted.

Saying goodbye to my son and Rhonda is never easy, but I'm a traveler. They're accustomed to me leaving so that I can become better for both them and the world. I told very few people I was going. I only told my best friends the day of.

My family wished me well. They were happy and inspired for what I was about to do. Actually, they seemed a bit envious. I certainly was very happy and tremendously inspired. Traveling to the unknown and documenting it is what movies and books are created from. You've got the book in your hands. A movie is coming.

As I got on my plane, I began to cry happy tears. I knew that the work I was about to do would not only be life-changing for me, but for others as well. I was going to do some major digging and share my treasures with the world. I was going with no expectations, no answers, just with an awakening and love in my heart. I would allow whatever experience, treasure or magic I experienced to present itself. I let go and trusted the process.

A Wandering Beginning

I arrived on January 6, just before noon. I'd found my Hostel, one referred to me by the director of the Maloka center. I settled in. But in a few hours I began to feel very weak. I developed a throbbing headache, rapid breathing and had no energy. What was happening to me? Those at the hostel knew—I was suffering from altitude sickness.

Cusco is over 11,000 feet above sea level. I was used to San Diego, nearly at sea level. The lower air pressure was affecting me. Though I normally hit the ground running, I was forced to stop and relax. I drank lots of water, took Tylenol and drank tea with coca leaves. It was all I could do.

After a nap, I was hungry. I made my way into Cusco on my own and found a market square. From there, I felt drawn down an alley to another, then down another until I came to a dead end. And there, as if waiting for me, was a place to eat.

The Shaman Vegan Restaurant sounded perfect—I wanted to eat vegan on this trip. I wanted to eat as clean as possible so that I could better connect with myself. I was the only person there. I sat, checked out the place, and noticed a poster.

On that poster was the gentleman in the canoe from the video I had watched a few days earlier. I was in the right place. And the meal was fantastic, the energy just what I wanted. I started feeling better again.

I investigated the town a little but my energy and head were still an issue. Somehow, after getting lost several times, I found my hostel. I slept most of the day; I had no energy to journal. I was being asked to take a timeout—no distractions, no hurry. Simply unplug and honor that.

I stayed in bed all the next day. All I could do was drink water and tea, and meditate. This wasn't fun, but needed. On the third day, I felt well enough to go back to the restaurant and ask about the gentleman in the canoe.

One of the staff told me she would call him. After a few words, she handed me the phone. A voice said, "Hello." The universe was working very fast.

His name was Mallku. He and his wife, Alanna, conducted spiritual journeys all over Peru. I thought that since I had no return scheduled, I might join one of his groups. I told him of my hiking plans, leaving two days from now.

He said that they lived not too far from his restaurant. Which was? "You're in it," he said. I couldn't help but smile. I'd just found out about him five days ago. I'd flown 3,500 miles and the first restaurant I ate in was his. Manifestation is a beautiful thing. We would meet the next day, at four.

I was so grateful. Something beautiful was going to happen—it already had. Mallku was going to meet me and provide the guidance I was seeking, with no expectation. I could feel a major shift in energy. It was about to get very real, very quick. I could hardly sleep. But I knew I needed rest. I was about to make a 26-mile trek up, and down, a mountain with all my gear on my back.

Back at the restaurant, I ate while I waited. My heart was in my throat. When he walked in, my heart settled again. Here was a man that exuded energy—a force both very powerful and loving. The polarity of male and female energy. He came over to me and said, "Tony?" We shook hands. "How can I help you?"

I told him the story of my last fifteen years. I outlined my experiences, my talents and my passions. I told him my need to find my purpose had consumed me for some time—positively, I added. I'd come to Peru to discover what might become the next chapter of my life: my legacy.

"Why am I here?" I asked.

Mallku said, "Life is a series of cycles. From the time you're born until you're about 7, you have the umbilical energetic cord with mother. Until 13, you begin to discover the world and the elements and confront nature. Up until 18, you search for social recognition to become an adult and begin accepting your independence. Up until 33, you're putting that into practice, testing it in professional and emotional ways. Until 49, you begin to realize what you want in life, in all aspects. 50 and beyond is the discovery of harmony between material life and spiritual life. This is the time of wisdom."

I began to understand why I was at this stage in my life. Wisdom was what I needed. And I needed to share it with the world. I would spend the rest of my life offering what I'd learn. This excited me.

This book is just the tip of the iceberg.

We spent a good hour together. We were like old friends. We were both 50 years old and respected one another. When two people connect after being spiritually connected, it's easy.

After going over my plans for the next several days, he told me to enjoy my journey, savor it, and then rest. After, he said, he would plan something special for me. We exchanged email addresses.

I could barely hold back my tears of joy. However, my smile shone. I knew the next two weeks would be epic.

Energy back to normal, I could finally enjoy Cusco. I wanted to explore its markets, the shops, the restaurants, the people, everything. And I loved the churches. This place embraced me and I would soon learn what it was that caused this feeling. Love was everywhere. Beauty was everywhere. I was so grateful to be here at this moment in my life. I was ready for more.

A Better Place

I moved from the hostel into the hotel that was part of my excursion package. This one had running hot water, a big bed, and was really clean. My plan was to rise at 3 a.m. to board a van for the drive to the entrance of the Inca trail. It was going to be a long day—the hike to the campsite was eight hours long.

I dedicate each day to a particular word. Today's word was "focus." Every step I took, I would stay focused, like the Incas had over 500 years ago. I recalled the times in my life when I had focused and what had resulted. I wanted everyone else that was taking the journey to find focus in their lives too. When you focus, you find, you create, and you conquer.

With each step, I was about to conquer doubt. As we approached the camp, I began to feel connected to nature. I heard the sound of water off in the distance, saw the occasional butterfly, and heard the birds sing. I felt that Mother Earth talked to me and showed me her beauty.

Exhausted, we arrived at the site around five. There were, in all, nine of us plus fifteen porters. The porters, carrying all our necessities, set up camp for us. I had my own tent.

I took off my shoes, happy to have that heavy backpack off my back, and took in the magnificent view. But I was beat. After eating, I settled in for the night.

The second day was the most intense. We were to cross Dead Woman's Pass, a three hour hike up 14,000 feet, and back down for four more hours. Going down is not easy. You really have to focus to stay safe, especially when the rain and wind hits. I dedicated this day to the word "health."

I knew that my health would have to be fully present to survive the day. With each step, I was grateful I had my health and that at the young age of 50, I was still able to manage such a difficult trek and actually enjoy it. I sent a prayer to the rest of the world, saying health is something each of us should honor more. Health is all that matters in life. Without health, you don't have a good quality of life. For that reason, life is health. As we rolled into camp exhausted and excited, I once again, in silence, acknowledged my health to the universe.

My face swelled so much on day three, I barely recognized myself. I had bags and rings under my eyes. I don't remember falling asleep and I didn't know where I was when I got up.

Apparently, I should have drank more water and kept my face out of the sun. But this would be an easier day than the previous two. After breakfast, we headed out to our final camp. We all felt more energetic. We'd proven ourselves. This day was dedicated to "love."

I felt so much love from those who knew I was on this journey and from those I'd just met. I wanted every step to send love out to the world—to all those that needed it, sought it or wanted to feel it. I thought about my loving wife who allowed me to do this. She had allowed me to discover love for myself, unselfishly. I sent my love back to her.

We made camp in the early afternoon. This gave us time to explore an Inca ruin not ten minutes away. Llamas roamed freely around the massive structure. Llamas are honored, power animals. The Andeans would look them in the eyes and offer gratitude. This was the animal of prosperity. They were beautiful, ran wild, and many times walked the trail with us. What a wonderful life experience.

After dinner, we went to bed. We had a 3 a.m. start facing us. A coming checkpoint would require us to wait in line while all those on the trail were accounted for. Sleeping was a challenge, but we needed it.

The scenery was spectacular, a full moon lighting up the distant mountains. Headlamps made us look like aliens—maybe we were—all trekking down to the checkpoint. After going through, we had a two-hour hike to the Sun Gate—the entrance to Machu Picchu. Oh, this day was dedicated to "discovery."

After everything I'd been through, I was about to discover an amazing sacred city. This was a big one for me. With every step, I wished that others could take their next step of discovery. I believe that the remaining time in our lives should be in the pursuit of discovery.

Day four was the most emotional. Even from a distance, I could feel the city's energy. She called to me; emotions could not be controlled. Many times, I just let it flow and found myself stopping to take in the stones beneath my feet, the butterflies that now seemed to be everywhere, and the clouds which crept up the mountains as the warm air pulled them to the peaks. Then someone cried out, "I see the Sun Gate. I see it!" We had arrived.

The Gift

To reach the gate, you have to climb 50 steps. They're hundreds of years old. The gate itself is a square arch. I found it hard to focus. Going up, I was emotional, disoriented.

I remember stepping through the gate and looking down on Machu Picchu and feeling an accomplishment far greater than any marathon or challenge I had ever faced. I had reached one of the most sacred places on earth. My life's meaning was gradually exposing itself to me. This place was to be the beginning.

Once inside, I failed to find the proper words to describe it. I even stopped taking pictures. There was no way to capture its magic.

Tourists flooded the city. They were fresh, clean, kids trailing, and pointing cameras everywhere. I hadn't showered in four days. I must say, going to Machu Picchu by bus greatly dilutes the experience. The trail gives you a much healthier appreciation for the magnitude of the city and its history. I know many want to see places fast and easy, and comfortable.

Machu Picchu is not one of those places. Step by step is the way.

The flood of people made me want to leave. The crush was overwhelming, to say the least. I was part of a group of nine among hundreds of milling tourists. I was glad to be able to stay an extra day and climb Huayna Picchu. That's the steep mountain you see in the background of the pictures of Machu Picchu. I would make my offering to the world the next morning.

I left my group early, thanking them for impacting my life so positively, then headed down to a city called Aguas Calientes, about a 30-minute drive by bus.

After checking into my hostel, I sat and thought about what had transpired. I was grateful for the experience. I could wait to go out tomorrow and finish what I'd set out to do.

I got up at four in the morning, gathered my tickets and passport—I needed those to get in again—and went down in plenty of time to get my bus. Some go in from Aguas Calientes, nearly a two-hour walk. But I was walked out.

I took my time. I didn't need to get to the checkpoint until seven. To my consternation, there were 500 already in line. No way would I make it through that line, up the hill and to the checkpoint in time. My heart told me to start walking.

I took off at a brisk pace for the base of the mountain. This wasn't my plan. But plans have to change if the need arises. Remember, I was a master at changing plans.

At the base, I met a Brazilian footballer. Since I was ill-prepared—I had no water—he said he'd share his. He was in great shape. This was going to be a quick hike.

He was doing this for his mother and family back home. They would never have the opportunity to see Machu Picchu themselves. I told him my story and we shed a few tears together as we climbed, passing everyone. We were on a mission.

We arrived at the Crystal City entrance in an hour and six minutes. That might be a record. Since I'd already been there and we had time, I gave him a tour of the different centers that I had experienced the day before.

We came to a sacred temple. I told him to come over and hold his hand six inches from a specific rock. You could feel energy from this rock raise the hair off your arm. It makes your fingers tingle. He fell to his knees and started crying. It was such a beautiful moment. He felt his mom was with him, along with his brothers and sisters. He apologized. I told him never to apologize when you feel love. We hugged each other and made our way to Huayna Picchu, which is another straight-up ascent to a summit.

This would take us about 45 minutes. Each step was dedicated to the word "gift." I was soon to be at the top and make an offering to the world. My gift from my journey. At the top, my friend and I parted. He'd found a perch, as I did. He knew what I was about to do and gave me the space to do it. He also needed some time alone. I had about an hour before my scheduled time and thought about what I would offer the world.

At 10 a.m. this is what I sent out to all those who needed it:

"I come here today to offer a message of love.

A message to all those needing mending.

A message that penetrates the shield we put up to protect ourselves.

For those that are searching may this offering show them the way.

For those hurting whether it be physical, mental, or spiritual.

May this message ease and remove the disease.

I come here today on my journey to inspire others to embrace a journey of their own.

To spend time with self, in deep thought listening to their hearts, not their minds.

May this message be accepted here at the most sacred of places on our planet to all those seeking a sign.

My deepest hope is that the communities we live in are lit up by the light in each of us and that the more we love, the brighter our present and future.

Today I come here as a man with these three thoughts: more gratitude, more beauty and more love.

I gift this offering to the universe, to all the creatures Mother has assembled from the elements: air, water, fire and earth.

I traveled many miles and came here to give this gift to the world.

May it be well received.

I am consumed with gratitude, surrounded by your beauty.

Inspired by your love."

TL

I left my perch, climbed down the mountain ready to go back to Cusco and begin what would be a four-day period that showed me what I wanted to see. Mallku would be my guide, my teacher and my friend.

20

Born Again

"Death is a reminder that we need to live."

Mallku sent me an email detailing our itinerary. Instead of joining one of his retreats as another member, there would only be the two of us for the entire four days. What an honor!

I called Rhonda, nearly jumping through the phone—I was so excited. So many things had to align—my schedule, his schedule, much more—to make this work. The universe obviously wanted this connection to happen, and fast.

The night before felt like Christmas Eve. I couldn't fall asleep. I couldn't think. But Mallku had everything under control. All I needed was my backpack, some food, my journal and toiletries.

We met at his restaurant at nine in the morning and immediately headed away from the city to a place called Moray. The Andeans believe Moray is the birthplace of Mother Earth (Pachamama). Moray is also the home of a powerful Inca site with large circular terraces. It was an utterly amazing area.

For our first ceremony, Mallku took me to a tucked-away power center so I could be truly immersed in its magical experience.

I Felt Me

I sat comfortably, my eyes closed, as Mallku guided the meditation. Focusing on my breath, embracing the moment, I allowed Pachamama to share her beauty with us by way of sound, wind and scent. Tears rolled down my face. I felt the peace and love of this sacred place.

Mallku instructed me to place my left hand on the ground and feel the earth—truly connect with it and its energy. My hand began to vibrate uncontrollably then move side to side. He then asked me to turn my right palm towards the sun. Instantly I felt the heat, its energy moving through my right palm down my body and out my left hand to the earth.

I had made a connection to both heaven and earth, my body tingling from head to toe. More tears. This was a love I'd never felt before—a love of Pachamama and myself. My divine was entwined with the divine Mother Earth.

I was liberated.

When we finished, Mallku gave me a gift that resembled a very small totem pole carved with the faces of two idols symbolizing the perfect balance of male and female energies.

You honor this symbol. It's Pachakamaq, the spirit that controls the forces of the universe and Pachamama. The winds that blow, the tides that rise and fall are all governed by Pachakamaq. It's the governor of all things, the supreme being and lord of the universe.

I accepted his gift, admired it and thanked Mallku for his generosity. I told him that I felt my life was a movie and I was the writer, director, producer and actor all at once. He liked that. We laughed about how the movie was going to have a great ending.

Our next stop was the city of Chinchero. We had to hike a long way, to some huge rocks of limestone that look like white lava with many holes and crevices—very abstract.

Mallku explained we were entering Pachamama's brain—that's what it looks like from above. Further into the brain, there were amazing cutouts shaped like chairs. They were the altars used by the masters to do their work through meditation. You could feel the energy come through the massive rocks. We offered gratitude for being there and requested permission to enter.

Mallku, a master guide, pointed out things that 95 percent of the visitors would probably miss. I felt privileged, knowing that I got to learn more than most. Then we came to a section of rock that, when I first saw it, shocked me.

The opening was shaped like a vagina—very distinctive. We were at the entrance to her bed. Mallku entered first to make an offering. After he was done, I would go inside after giving reverence.

When he returned, I could barely get my feet moving. I was extremely emotional. Once inside I began to cry like a child. I kissed each of the walls and simply stayed there, my hands still on the walls, as the tears continued. I can't put into words the love I felt—I won't even try. But I hope everyone, just for a moment, feels love this powerful.

When I was done, I found Mallku had climbed to a huge altar-shaped cutout. This was the altar of the Snake, Puma and Kondor, the three most powerful animals of the Andes.

He invited me to sit quietly in the cutout for 18 minutes. I wanted more than 18, but I adhered to his request. Here, I felt the perfect balance of power and love, the perfect polarity of Pachamama, the male and the female, the Yin and the Yang.

Back at his restaurant, we gave thanks for this special moment in time. Pachamama's brain and bed were truly singular. The day had changed me. I felt love. I felt a connection. I felt me.

Mallku and I shared a great meal and a glass of grapes to celebrate our time together.

Tomorrow promised even more. For that I was excited. I went to bed with an open mind, heart and soul.

Our first stop was Tipon. It was here we discovered the place where heaven and Earth connect. At the base of the mountain a stream comes up from the earth. The entire area had an aroma of purity. The air was so crisp and clean you could almost taste it with every breath.

The sun was perfect, very few clouds in the sky—a beautiful morning. We meditated with our shoes off to connect fully with this sacred power place. After two minutes, I felt I had to move. I did, and heard the sound of running water over rocks.

Instantly tears rolled down my face. I was overwhelmed with the sound and air. It was like I was being cleansed. I stayed 18 minutes before moving on.

At a waterfall, we sat and Mallku made an offering. Then we reached into the crisp water and washed our hands and faces. He invited me to sit with him and take in the moment as he guided me to fully embrace this place.

With our eyes closed, he described that we wanted this water to flow from here and to cleanse everything it came in contact with as it flowed out to the rivers and the tributaries to meet up with the Amazon river—the mightiest river in the world—and eventually flow into the ocean. He asked that this water be accepted by the clouds in the form of rain, and that it rain to cleanse and purify the places that needed it. As soon as he said that, a gentle rain began to fall.

It was light enough that it didn't disturb that powerful moment. I turned my right palm to the sky and felt as if the heavens where sending the rain to cleanse me through that hand. Water was moving through me and out my feet back into the earth. This connection brought on more tears. I could feel them leave my face and fall into the stream below. It was a very special time.

As soon as we were done, the rain stopped. Mallku said that Pachamama was showing us her beauty. It was an event I will hold dear forever. I know he will too.

Pisaq came next. This place is truly massive. Hundreds of holes are carved into the mountain. It looks like a beehive, but it's a cemetery. Death was honored here. Every morning, the sun offers light to those that have moved on.

We found a spot on a balcony—the sun and a natural pyramid off in the distance. Mallku once again invited me to sit with him for 18 minutes. This was a place of forgiveness. I was to use my quiet time to forgive—forgive all those that affected me, those that I affected and most importantly, forgive myself.

Once again, I had to let go in order to grow. The cleansing from today made me feel that I could float. We headed back to Cusco and I found myself in a place of peace that I had never been before. I admired Mallku for all the work he had done in his life. He shared his knowledge, wisdom and passion freely. And he's impacted thousands over the years through his books and sacred journeys.

Becoming a Kondor

The third day is one I'll never forget. A few days before, I'd told Mallku of a vision I'd had when climbing Machu Picchu.

I'd climbed Huayna Picchu, and near the summit I'd met my wife. We'd kissed and climbed to the summit, hand in hand. There, she'd let go. She'd smiled but tears welled up.

There was a stone stairway leading to the sun, nothing but open sky on both sides. I took each step slowly.

Halfway up, a voice said, "Tony you've journeyed so far. You've never given up and you continue to inspire the world with your light. You've always glided, you've always taught, you've always embraced knowledge. And you continue to fly no matter the circumstances. Remember, as a child you looked to the heavens, fascinated with the stars and sun."

I said, "Yes."

"Also, remember the time you wore a towel around your neck as a cape thinking you could fly?"

"Yes."

"Remember your fascination with flight, airplanes, birds, and falling rain? Or the time you drove two hours to get to the airport in Hawaii so you could feel what it was like to fly in a glider?"

"Yes."

"You even took lessons to get a pilot's license."

"Yes."

"As you got older, you wanted to jump off high bridges into the water below just to feel flight, if only for a minute."

"Yes."

"You would watch pelicans hover inches above the water, gliding for hours with no effort."

"Yes."

"You always speak of freedom and discovering your power."

"Yes."

"Tony, you're the chosen one, my most majestic of all creations. You've been guided your whole life by me, Pachamama, and Wiraqocha and Pachakamaq. Together, we've brought you here and you're now a Kondor. In all the universe, there's no other animal that stands for all that you are. Your wings are strong and wide enough to carry all those that need to transcend to discover their light. You can fly into the sun as your flight knows no limit. We welcome you into our brotherhood. You are a Kondor!"

I didn't even know what a Kondor was and now I'm one? Mallku simply smiled and said, "That's good."

Today, Mallku had a surprise for me. He took me to a sanctuary for rescued kondors. They could glide about in a safe place to rest and recover. First the vision and now this!

Their wings can be over ten feet, tip to tip, making it the largest bird by weight and wingspan combined. We got to observe these majestic animals close up, took pictures and just connected with them. I was in awe, to say the least. To be in this sanctuary with them and have them walk up to you, spread their wings, gaze at you as you lay in the grass with them, was simply one of the most powerful things I have ever experienced.

I thanked Mallku for this life-changing event and allowing me to experience all this grandeur. It's very cool to be a Kondor.

Connected

After, we visited a place that's, from a power perspective, the second most powerful on Earth. Only the Great Pyramid of Giza has more energy. Along the way, he suggested I write a book.

This after I'd told him that I had another vision in which I saw the book's subject, how it was divided, its intent and purpose. I knew more details would present themselves eventually. But for now, I was excited that Pachamama had shown me the book I was to write and how it would affect the lives of millions.

All this made Mallku smile. He's authored several books. I knew his insights would help me to write mine.

Saqsaywaman (pronounced almost like *sexy-woman*) is a place that, when you first visit, words just don't leave your mouth. The site is breathtaking. Stones cut with unbelievable precision, many over 25 feet tall, perfect in shape, are fitted together like an intricate puzzle.

The Masters would come here to gain their wisdom and honor Pachamama. Without getting into the technical aspects of this place, it was perfect in design and placement with regards to the sun and stars. It's a magical place. From Saqsaywaman, you can look down on the city of Cusco.

It was here that Mallku answered the questions I'd had a few days earlier about how to meditate properly. These I will outline at the end of the book so you can understand and use these skills too—ones you must embrace.

On the grass, we did 18 minutes of reverence. The whole time, I was thinking how I'd share all my experiences with the world. This book is only the first step.

Later, we visited Amaru Machay, known as the Cave of the Serpents. We explored the caves and their unique rock formations. I even did the walking ceremony with my eyes closed so I could feel and trust Pachamama.

This day was one that I would share over and over again. The power and beauty needed to be shared and felt.

On my last day with Mallku, we did our Wachuma ceremony. Wachuma, also referred erroneously to as San Pedro, is a cactus plant with wonderful healing properties. I heard about this ceremony when I was in Peru doing Ayahuasca.

Wachuma is the best way to explain a deep connection with Pachamama. The effects are normally not as intense as Ayahuasca, but can sometimes be. The intent is to allow you to have a deeper connection with yourself and your relationship with Pachamama. In preparation, I had to fast for eight hours—hence no breakfast that day.

We went to a remote power center a few miles from the city. The weather was perfect, the air crisp. Mallku said a blessing for the ceremony and gave me a cup with the equivalent of an overflowing shot of liquid. I gave a moment of gratitude and stated my intent for the ceremony.

Wachuma's effect was subtle. I felt very alert and noticed every little thing—bugs, sounds and the voice of the trees. I found a tree—the largest in the area and right in the middle of the forest—that had been somewhat abused. It was discolored and some of its bark was missing. I was drawn to the size and the discolorations. I walked up and admired its proportions, colors, strength and beauty. I hugged it and held it close to me, like the welcome you give a friend you've not seen in ten years. I even kissed it and truly sent my loving energy for the longevity and the stories this tree must have. I simply honored it and acknowledged its greatness. It was a beautiful creation from the earth.

Afterwards, we went to a very unique forest that featured Eucalyptus trees—just a few rows of them. The Eucalyptus tree is not native to Peru.

This small forest separates the power centers in the area. It's a very special place. As we entered, I was immediately brought back to my childhood, growing up in California. I lived in trees like these. I'd get lost running from George. The Eucalyptus trees were my safety net. They were my old friends. Mallku invited me to spend ten minutes with whatever tree resonated with me and simply honor it—the branches, the leaves, the roots, the soil. To be present.

After, Mallku walked me to another power center. There were a couple of altars there: one fit for a king, another much smaller. Mallku suggested I sit in the one I was drawn to while he explored further. I chose the kingly one—and felt like one.

Mallku invited me to stay for 18 minutes and connect. I sat back and offered my gratitude and began what I had learned yesterday. Within moments I felt Wachuma shine a bright light on me. I was about to feel something very special—and I did.

This light was the whitest I have ever seen. I pushed myself back into the altar as if I was descending into a tunnel. I went farther and farther and farther backwards, the light still bright, completely at peace with what was happening.

Mallku returned and spoke a mantra welcoming us back from our 18 minutes. During our walk home, he said that we were there for over an hour. I had no idea.

Walking back through the forest, Mallku asked that I pick a tree and say goodbye. I picked a different one this time. Again, I honored my time while giving love to this tree in the form of a hug, touch and even a few heartfelt kisses.

By this time, Mallku had walked to the car. I was a few moments behind. Then I looked down and saw it—the reason

I'd come to Cusco, the reason that I had been put in different situations for over 50 years, many very difficult. It was a reminder of who I was and will always be. I will share this ultimate gift with you in the next chapter. But for now, stay as I share with you my birth.

Breaking Free

Holding on to this gift, tears in my eyes, Mallku and I did not speak all the way back to the restaurant. He knew I'd experienced something special.

For the last half of our day, he'd planned to take me into the ceremonial center at the back of his restaurant. The moment I walked in, I felt I was in another power center. The colors, the energy, the feeling that was evident here was, in a word, magical.

Mallku said a few words about this space then asked that I find a comfortable place and make it my own. There were lots of blankets, pillows, stuffed tigers and puma. Shoes off, I sat in the corner. But I felt isolated. So I grabbed some blankets and a pillow and made myself a nest of sorts. I lay down and got really comfortable.

As he meticulously prepared the instruments needed for our ceremony, I gave thanks for being here. Once ready, he invited me to close my eyes, take a few deep breaths and let the experience in. I was at peace, I was happy and I trusted Mallku.

Mallku orchestrated a symphony using a sound bowl, chimes, whistles and a few other things.

I drifted to another place. On my back, I began to get uneasy. I didn't like this position, so I sat up in a meditation pose and felt myself begin to sway. In a moment or two, my head dropped to my chest. I couldn't hold it up. I was in the shape of an egg.

The music got louder, the beat stronger, more intense. I felt trapped. I needed to get out of this—whatever I was in. The music got louder and I looked around—it was completely dark. I was inside a shell of some sort—an egg. I needed to get out!

With every bit of force I could muster, I extended my left hand as strongly as I could. I did the same with my right, punching out hard. My arms were now free. I started moving my head side to side. Eventually my head poked through. Finally, I had broken free of my shell.

I put out my right foot and put weight on it. But my leg shook and wobbled uncontrollably. It was very weak. My left leg did the same thing. I flapped my arms like a bird to give me balance then put more weight on my feet. I went very slowly, adding even more weight. My legs shook badly. I flapped for balance.

Somehow I figured out a way to stand. I used my arms for balance and occasionally flapped for stability. I looked around.

My arms were wings, not full with feathers but beautiful all the same. I admired them and the perch I stood on. I heard the sound of wings flapping—very powerful wings, wings from a huge bird. Only one bird was capable of making a sound that powerful. A Kondor.

My teacher was teaching me how to fly. To get more wind under my wings, I flapped them in a big sweeping motion, attempting to mimic the speed and sound of my teacher. I flapped faster and faster, and jumped at the same time. Kondors need a little jump to make room for their wings and get the wind underneath them. I jumped quickly, powerfully, and flapped my wings like I was on fire. The music grew louder and louder just as I was ready to lift. But I felt a tug at my left leg. There was a lion holding me back.

The lion had gripped my leg and wanted to attack me. I flapped harder still, jumped more. Faster and harder. My wings finally got the air they needed and I broke free. I'd broken from the lion I once was. I'd become the most powerful and majestic creature ever created.

I flew, gliding as a Kondor and soared over the valley below. Feeling the wind through my wings, I adjusted my flight to make it what I wanted. I was a Kondor. I could fly higher than any animal. My wings allowed me to take as many people as I wanted to the light.

The music stopped and Mallku said, "Welcome back." I stood in the middle of the floor, very solid, with my arms extended as far as they could. I realized what had just happened and collapsed, tears in my eyes.

I had been born again, my life forever changed. My purpose was detailed for me—I would spend the rest of my life assisting others to ascend to their light.

We spent the rest of the afternoon together, had a meal in the room and talked about what was next. We had both learned something. We discovered something new and got to share something very special.

He was my master guide. He'd been chosen to assist me. I was the one chosen to receive the final lessons to continue my mission to glide, sharing my wisdom. In our conversation, I asked Mallku what his name meant. With a smile on his face he simply said, "Mallku means the spirit of the Kondor, the leader of the peoples." In a sense, he is the leader and teacher of the Kondors.

It's wisdom you now possess.

You're holding the blueprint, process, strategy, guide and action steps to make whatever time you have on this earth adventurous, purposeful and rich.

My wish, and the wish of Pachakamaq, Wiraqocha and Pachamama, is that you honor yourself and your experiences, take responsibility and spend the rest of your days in the pursuit of discovery. Learn more about nature and the foods you eat. Become passionate not just about life, but truly *living* your life.

For our time together, I'm grateful. What you're about to do is simply beautiful, just like you.

On your journey you'll discover a love like no other because you'll find yourself. Now is the time to do the good.

Let go, trust and glide!

APPENDIX

How to Give Birth to a Kondor

The idea of giving birth to a Kondor is hardly the topic of everyday discussion. However, this book, one you've chosen, for which I'm grateful, is.

The path that each one of us is on, or has temporarily wandered from, in its awkwardness, frustration and constant questioning, is a beautiful thing. I love that you've found your way here. My guess is, you're *on* the path once again.

As we journey together and the words on these pages begin to resonate, you'll be asking yourself if this new path is even real? Is this even possible? Make no mistake, pass no judgement, you're beyond that now. You're on the brink of illumination. You're here, the conversations from yesterday gone, open to what's next, the message, and the confirmation of what you should do.

This book is the key to opening the door, flipping the switch, igniting your passion—pick your favorite metaphor. Every word is true. Every person, although their names may have been changed, can be verified. Every emotion and lesson that surfaced as my fingers, through a higher power, managed to somehow translate my 50-year journey to impact your life, has occurred.

I've documented it for you. I have done the work. Or, as I like to say, I've done the *good* for you. This is the gift you have manifested in your quiet time, that you wanted to be unveiled precisely at this moment.

This is a gift like no other. This is the guidance you've been waiting for. You're now awake enough to digest, study and apply the lessons learned at the end of each chapter, to put them to use and spend the remaining days of your life heading in the direction of your light.

A word of caution. Humans have the unique ability to want answers faster. They strive to find an easier way, to fast-forward, to get to the bottom line as quickly as possible and still stay comfortable in the process. Although I welcome this facility, to do that with this book would be a great travesty.

In life, I have learned to observe and take in each moment. There's magic in that. You won't know what chapter, page, paragraph, sentence or even what word is going to cause the layer of the onion to release the right aroma for you. The sequence of events could be the code that brings illumination. Or the sequence of letters. In them, you'll find what you're looking for. And I'm giving you the combination.

Sure, you'll know the next step, but now's not the time to zoom to the conclusion. I'm also wise enough to know that just when you think you've arrived, there's another bus to catch. Just when you think you've figured out the puzzle, you'll realize there's still a missing piece, hidden somewhere.

I'll continue to spend whatever time I have on this wonderful place called Earth in the pursuit of discovery, searching for the next piece. If you're not growing, moving or flapping your wings, you'll die along the way.

It has taken me 50 years to give birth to the person I am today. Before that, I was a Kondor in incubation, in an extended gestation period, hiding. I'm strong now. I fly higher than any other bird in existence. My wings are the largest in the world. I can carry those seeking the light.

I wait for the wind, I take it all in with gratitude, beauty and love in my heart. I leap and simply glide. No more worries, my friend. No more hesitation, fear, uncertainty or doubt. You've been searching and I have your message. Magnificence does exist; we need more of those willing to ascend into the light.

Get comfortable. Embrace this moment and let's glide.

Tony Lucero

My Greatest Gift

The image is one I captured on the final day of my journey with Mallku. Let me describe it and offer my interpretation along with a reminder of what really matters.

As a kid, I escaped from my stepfather by hiding in the Eucalyptus forest near my home in California. When I entered the forest in Cusco, some 43 years later, the smell immediately brought me back to that innocent child. This leaf reminds me to always stay in that childlike state.

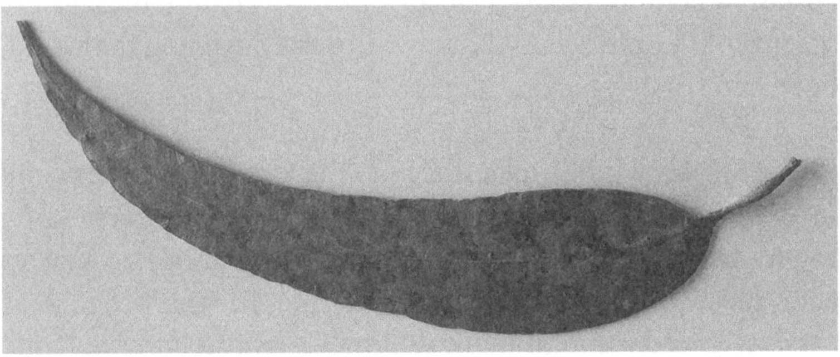

Those that know me will say I act like a teenager at times. I'm playful, always seeking fun. This leaf reminds me to stay young in my heart.

The red is unique; it really stood out when I saw it. It's a red with brown spots and discolorations. One spot resembles a heart.

I've always been, or felt, colorful. I've always acknowledged my heart. My clothes, my hair, my attitude, my voice have never been normal. The brown spots are the bruises I endured as a kid and throughout my life. Even today, life provides obstacles and some people want to derail us all. That color is a simple reminder to stay true to myself.

Be a person of color, one that stands out and doesn't hide behind the bruises of yesterday. Share them with the world.

The shape is that of a wing. Funny to now know that I'm a Kondor with mighty, beautiful wings. And finally, as I remember, I found it at the bottom of the last step before entering the forest. How could this leaf be so perfect? Hundreds of people come down into the forest; it's right there, ready for someone to crush it. Someone must have stepped on it. But yet, it's intact, has no flaws, perfect from tip to tip.

My whole life, even as a kid, I never believed what others told me. I'm sure there are many who don't understand me and wish to see me fail. In truth, I have failed, many times. And suffered trauma. But those misfortunes have helped me find the message. As many times as some have attempted to step on me, I have made it and I remain perfect. This perfect Eucalyptus leaf is me and my reminder of the simple things I was. In my simplicity, I have become a majestic Kondor. I was, and am, perfect!

So are you, despite your discolorations, your bumps and bruises. They're the divine. You are the light you seek. You were a perfect miracle when you were born and will always be perfect. You've always been guided and will continue to be as long as you know this: there is a plan for you and being awake allows you to stay on course.

Honor yourself daily, take nature walks, look to the stars and the moon and the sun for direction. Protect your environment so no one steps on you. Be more grateful, see the beauty that surrounds you.

And finally, love each moment, for that is truly your greatest gift.

My Gift to the World

"I come here today to offer a message of love.

A message to all those needing mending.

A message that penetrates the shield we put up to protect ourselves.

For those that are searching may this offering show them the way.

For those hurting whether it be physical, mental, or spiritual.

May this message ease and remove the disease.

I come here today on my journey to inspire others to embrace a journey of their own.

To spend time with self, in deep thought listening to their hearts, not their minds.

May this message be accepted here at the most sacred of places on our planet to all those seeking a sign.

My deepest hope is that the communities we live in are lit up by the light in each of us and that the more we love, the brighter our present and future.

Today I come here as a man with these three thoughts: more gratitude, more beauty and more love.

I gift this offering to the universe, to all the creatures Mother has assembled from the elements: air, water, fire and earth.

I traveled many miles and came here to give this gift to the world.

May it be well received.

I am consumed with gratitude, surrounded by your beauty.

Inspired by your love."

Tony Lucero 10 a.m. EST Jan 14, 2017

Living in Your Circles of Your Life

This is how to set up your day, end your day, and start manifesting. Follow the steps exactly. Be focused and purposeful while doing them. Consistency is key. You can apply this process anytime during the day, but doing them every morning is vital. Let's start designing your life.

Get a big (around 25 x 30 inches) poster board from your local office supply store. You need this much space to help you visualize. Hang it in your office, or on any wall.

Do this exercise daily with the following in mind:
YOU ARE WEALTHY! You have plenty of money in the bank; money is not an issue!!!

You should have NO limiting beliefs. Time to dream big! No limitations for what goes in each circle.

I need to say it again—YOU ARE WEALTHY!

On your poster board, create three big circles, edges touching. Label them: Experiences, Wellness, and Prosperity.

Each circle represents a very important area of your life.

Experiences

The experiences are those things you desire in your life: the exciting places, the house or houses, flying, skydiving, learning Spanish in Spain, a month-long vacation and where.

Include such things as: relationship(s), housekeeper, shopping sprees, type of car(s), wardrobe, attending a Super Bowl, front row or backstage to your favorite concert.

You get the idea. They are your *Lived List*. We want these experiences while we are living, not while we're waiting to die.

Wellness

This is your health and lifestyle circle.

What is your ideal weight, size and shape? What is your workout regimen like? Are you doing yoga? Running? Martial arts? How many days a week? Do you have a personal trainer? What type of meals are you eating—organic? Do you have a chef? Do you have a gym in your house? Are you taking walks with nature? How often? Any spiritual work? Meditation? Are you doing preventative care on your body? Massages? Facials? If so, how often?

Fill this circle with everything health related, anything that keeps your mind, body and spirit happy.

Prosperity

This interesting circle is a statement of your character and values.

This is more than being well-off financially; it's the pay-it-forward mentality that will enrich your life.

True prosperity is showing others the way. If you know something that can assist someone, offer your wisdom. With that being said, what are you doing with your time? Remember you're rich. Are you donating time to a church, tithing more? Start a foundation to support a cause your heart agrees with.

What's getting you out of bed in the morning? What's your legacy? From a financial aspect, how much money are you worth? How much of that is liquid? How much money do you have sitting in your bank account? How much do you want and by when?

When filling these circles, keep in mind these key points:

1. You must be *very specific*. It's one thing to want to go on a vacation, it's another to know where and when you're going, for how long and with whom. It's one thing to say you want to move. It's another to know when, where, the size of the house, color, style etc. The universe and the laws that govern manifestation need exact instructions. Be specific.

2. Create a feeling, frequency and vibration of what you're manifesting. Simply looking at these circles is NOT enough.

Sit yourself before them and visualize yourself walking through your dream home in a dream part of town, making supper or watching a movie, and creating a vibration while inside. That vibration is fuel for the Law of Manifestation.

Once it's felt, a reciprocal process begins. The more feeling, the more pronounced the frequency. I can tell you from experience that if you become emotional during this activity, if you truly see yourself experiencing everything in your circles, you'll be amazed by what will begin to happen. And now, since you're wide awake, you're beginning to understand its power.

This exercise should take more than just a few minutes.

There are times when it has taken me three days or more. What's in these circles are my thoughts, my dreams, my desires.

Don't just do this once. Spend time thinking about the circle's contents. Add to your circles as thoughts and ideas come up.

Every morning, sit before your circles of your life. Do it every night too. Sit before them for 10 minutes, 20, or just 5. But you must be purposeful and see yourself already experiencing your life as it unfolds in front of you.

Be CONSISTENT!

Taking a Time Out

I want to go deeper into the idea of meditation. Spending time with yourself, just yourself, has many benefits. It doesn't matter how you get that time alone, but that you use it wisely.

This is the part of that day that I hold sacred and honor with the highest of respect. I truly honor myself and my greatest commodity—time.

Many go into this quiet time looking for quick answers. For many years I did that too, until I was guided to understand how to master this most treasured of practices.

What I'm about to share with you is how to master honoring your quiet time. I'll use the word *meditation* for the rest of what I'm describing. Don't get hung up on the word. I've called it Tony time, selfish time, prayer, time out and simply chill. Make this a discipline that becomes an extension of you. The world doesn't need to *medicate*; it needs to *meditate.*

Set a vibrating alarm for 18 minutes. This is the base time of your meditation. Why 18 minutes?

Five minutes are used up by the brain wanting to be your enemy as you attempt to settle in. Your schedule, your kids, work, did you take out the trash, is the door locked, did you check Facebook, and much more, show up during the first 5 minutes. Your mind loves chaos.

Get comfortable. You can lie down, sit up, cross your legs, whatever works. Remember, we like comfort. So, be comfortable.

During this time, breathe in deep through your nose, filling your diaphragm, not your lungs. You need to practice this. As you inhale, you should feel your stomach become full. Once full, very slowly exhale all the air through your mouth. Do this slowly and controlled. As random thoughts enter your mind, simply acknowledge them and focus on breathing. Again this is a focused practice. As you get closer to the 5 minute mark, you'll begin to notice that the outside noises diminish.

With practice, as soon as you set the stage to meditate, your mind will honor this time and find somewhere else to play. This is your time. Be patient and do not get discouraged with the chatter.

You'll know, roughly, when the 5 minutes are up.

The next 10 minutes are the magical minutes, or sweet spot. This is when the conscious side of your brain gets bored and goes quiet.

The subconscious side of your brain is now in control. All you need to do is focus on your breathing. If a stray thought enters, refocus your attention to your breathing. During this time, you may notice a humming in your head or in your ears. This is your frequency.

Tune into that frequency while you continue to breathe. This should go on for about 10 minutes. As you practice, you'll hear a kind of static noise very clearly. This is good. You're tuning in. Stay and enjoy this quiet time. Do not force anything. Your goal now is peace, quiet and honoring. The answers you seek will not come from meditation's quiet time, but come later, in your awake time.

The magic of quiet time is the creation of space for the answers to come. You could be working out, cleaning, shopping, reading and all of sudden you get this unavoidable strong feeling to do something. Congratulations, this is the benefit of meditation.

The last 3 minutes are spent asking for guidance, answers, healing or whatever you want clarified. Usually, during this time, you're more alert. If I'm lying down for the first part of the meditation, I'll sit up for the last 3 minutes—this changes the energy. At this time, acknowledge yourself, your guides, spirits, God, Pachamama and offer gratitude and love for this very special time. I also ask for direction, for a sign to be shown or felt, in order for me to do something. If there's someone or something I need to experience, please allow that connection to be made when the time is right.

The important thing to remember, as with everything you have learned, is your intention. Be open to the benefits of doing meditation. When you meditate daily, without expectation, the unexpected happens.

Remember, 18 minutes is your base. Can it be more? Yes, absolutely. If you go 30, 45 or more, that's wonderful. Whatever time you need to honor, is what you should do. But always complete the minimum 18.

I love to start my day with meditation. The evening, before winding down for bed, works for me too.

It's a beautiful thing.

A Few Final Words

There are different ways to spell terms and place names used in this book.

- Ayahuasca can also be written as Ayawaska
- Huayna Picchu can also be written as Wayna Pijchu
- Machu Picchu can also be written as Machu Pijchu
- Kondor can also be written as Condor. It has been modified over the years as many cities in Peru changed letters in their names

Reminders

1. Choice
2. Change
3. Music
4. Follow your gut
5. Find a mentor
6. Law of manifestation
7. List of your talents, skills and personality
    - Your culture
    - Your attitude
    - S.O.U. (Sense of Urgency)
8. Fuel your body
9. Become passionate about growth
    - Read 15-30 pages, daily minimum
    - Remove clutter
    - Protect your environment
10. Challenge yourself
11. Discover love
12. Do you have someone guiding you?
13. Forgiveness
14. Heal yourself
15. Follow your heart
16. Meditate

Kondor Notes

Kondor Notes